MEMORY INTO MEMOIR

ALSO BY LAURA KALPAKIAN

*The Unruly Past: Memoirs*

*The Great Pretenders*

*Three Strange Angels*

*The Music Room*

*A Christmas Cordial and Other Stories*

*Unspoken Truths*

*American Cookery*

*The Memoir Club*

*Educating Waverley*

*The Delinquent Virgin: Novella and Stories*

*Steps and Exes*

*Caveat*

*Graced Land*

*Dark Continent and Other Stories*

*Cosette: A Sequel to Les Misérables*

*Fair Augusto and Other Stories*

*Crescendo*

*These Latter Days*

*Beggars and Choosers*

LAURA KALPAKIAN

# MEMORY INTO MEMOIR

*a writer's handbook*

University of New Mexico Press | Albuquerque

© 2021 by Laura Kalpakian
All rights reserved. Published 2021
Printed in the United States of America

Library of Congress Cataloging-in-Publication Data
Names: Kalpakian, Laura, author.
Title: Memory into memoir : a writer's handbook /
    by Laura Kalpakian.
Description: [Albuquerque, New Mexico]:
    University of New Mexico Press, 2021.
Identifiers: LCCN 2021020076 (print)
    LCCN 2021020077 (e-book)
    ISBN 9780826363114 (paperback) |
    ISBN 9780826363121 (e-book)
Subjects: LCSH: Autobiography—Author-
    ship. | Biography as a literary form.
Classification: LCC PE1479.A88 K35 2021 (print)
    LCC PE1479.A88 (e-book)
    DDC 808.06/692—dc23

LC record available at https://lccn.loc.gov/2021020076
LC e-book record available at https://lccn.loc.gov/2021020077

Cover Images | Old map © Jules Kitano | istockphoto.com
    Sledding in New Hampshire © Mindy Basinger Hill
    Old newspaper © Mindy Basinger Hill
    Old photos © michellegibson | istockphoto.com
    Handwriting | MAXSHOT | istockphoto.com
Designed by Mindy Basinger Hill
Composed in Parkinson Electra Pro
    and Uniform Ultra Condensed

*This book is for*

PEGGY KALPAKIAN JOHNSON

A *heroine to her children,*

*her grandchildren,*

*and her great-grandchildren*

*And the heroine of this book*

# Contents

# Prologue

S ince I think metaphorically and anecdotally, I believe there is a
story for everything. And so, there is a story for this book.

My fascination with the memoir goes back to when I was twelve
and very much entranced with eighteenth-century America. In our
small storefront public library I found a series of social histories about
colonial America written in the early 1900s by a New England author,
Alice Morse Earle. At the back of each book she listed her sources,
many of which were eighteenth-century diaries, memoirs, and collections of letters, all published as books, but certainly not available
in our little library. My mother suggested I try interlibrary loan, and
behold! There came to Southern California from some far, far away
New England library, *The Diary of Anna Green Winslow: A Boston
Schoolgirl of 1771*, edited by Alice Morse Earle. Though Anna Green
Winslow was not without spirit, her 1771 diary was far more pious
than I had hoped. Still, she spoke to me across the centuries, and for
that reason alone, her diary was enchanting. Thus began my lifelong
affection for, and interest in, voices long past.

Probably that's why I was a history major for both an undergraduate
degree at a university close to home and a master's degree at a university on the east coast. I returned to California—admittedly, to live
by the beach—and got into a prestigious grad school where I worked
toward a PhD in literature. Students in this program chose concen-
trations in a genre, an author, and an era (these last two could not
overlap). Charles Dickens was my author, and the Great War (World
War I) was my era, and for genre I chose memoir and autobiography.

Friday afternoons I would go to the library with a big satchel and
roam the stacks, choosing memoirs, autobiographies, books of letters,
and journals. As I sank into these pages, I found, then as now, that the

books I like best are not, say, the sonorous three volumes of Henry James's recollections, or Henry Adams's magisterial prose, but the books by often obscure people who put their lives on paper, pioneers, travelers, long-forgotten theatrical types, artists, abolitionists, educators, cooks, poets, plural wives, people who in rendering their experience might whine or guffaw upon the page, who had genuine voices.

Aside from copious reading, graduate school also afforded me the opportunity to teach Freshman Composition—great training for a writer, which, by then, was my ambition, kept secret from all but a very few friends. Two days a week, I toiled away at my own writing. Weekends I had a retail job. Three days a week I went to campus, took classes, and taught Freshman Comp. I liked teaching Freshman Comp. With every essay, I had to ask the writer's core question: What makes good writing? Over several years (and with the usual blood, sweat, and tears), I learned to answer that question. In fact, I'm still learning to answer it. I did not get the PhD, but I did become a novelist.

Later, I was honored to be the Roethke Writer-in-Residence at the University of Washington where I taught English 581, "The Writer as Critical Reader," required for MFA students. I was told I could fill the English 581 syllabus with anything I wanted (even My Favorite Books—tempting). But I took this opportunity to revel in my passion for autobiography and prose memoirs. English 581 was the most demanding class I ever taught. The reading was ambitious unto formidable: for a ten-week term, ten separate texts, some of them dense and difficult. The first batch began with *The Education of Henry Adams*, *The Autobiography of W. E. B. Dubois*, and *All God's Dangers: The Life of Nate Shaw* (each of these about five hundred pages long). On reserve at the library (and thus, all in one place) was a resource list, one hundred-some-odd books, mostly classic British and American memoirs. For finals students gave an oral presentation about an author of their choice, wrote a paper about that author—oh, and each wrote a personal memoir as well. These eager MFA students leapt into the material, making every class exciting, even exhilarating, a never-to-be-forgotten experience.

In the following decades teaching memoir classes, writing groups, and independent edits, I have supported probably hundreds of writers through the process of transforming memory into memoir. I have helped them bring to narrative fruition the memories they carry in their heads and hearts. My immersion in the memoir deepened as I watched writers evoke the elusive past on the page, and animate the people in that past, to make the experience vivid for a reader outside the self. That's what memoir aspires to.

Both memoir and fiction rely on imagination. Writing a memoir is not simply an act of preservation, but an act of invention, because the fabric of the past is never clean, hemmed, pressed, folded, and stacked chronologically. The past comes to us in fragments finished off by imagination. Indeed, memoir best flourishes at the confluence of memory and imagination: memory calls on imagination to mend the ragged ends, to create continuity over the frayed parts. In transforming amorphous memory into narrative memoir, the writer puts a literary structure over the past, hoping to both capture and evoke, one act propelling the other. This is the writing process, that is to say, the canopy concept over this book. *Memory into Memoir* is less of an Ikea how-to-assemble manual, and more of an invitation to reimagine the past in writing, to rethink, revisit memory in prose. *Memory into Memoir* explores the process of placing narrative form over the unruly past.

Prose does not spring onto the page like Venus on the half-shell. Writing is a process, of growth and change, and discovery. And, as I learned all those years ago in grad school—and still firmly believe—good writing is good writing, no matter the form. Memoir, fiction, nonfiction, narrative prose of any sort use the same tools—narration, dialogue, scenic depiction, dramatic arc, character development, vivid language. Memoir writers can learn from fiction, and fiction writers can profit from memoir. The materials you will find in this book, though specific to memoir, can be used by any writer. In *Memory into Memoir* I've shared my enthusiasm for certain poems and songs. I've included original materials and prompts, tactics refined over decades and chosen with care. Among the examples you'll find student memoirs that are not gorgeously groomed, but raw and in process; work, in other words, that can grow and deepen. For gorgeously groomed you'll find a list of all the books mentioned in these pages (many of which do qualify as My Favorite Books). These are not assigned as texts, but listed as resources for the writer who wants to delve further into the techniques, or the experience, of these authors. I've also used as illustration scenes culled from my own novels and stories. I've selected these rather than quoting others' work because I could (and did) edit my own work to suit the needs of *Memory into Memoir.*

As I now read (and reread, revise, and rethink) what I have written in this book I see that my own past plays a role here, making *Memory into Memoir* also a personal memoir of sorts. I've dedicated this book to my mother, Peggy Kalpakian Johnson, and followed her writing process in these pages because it is illustrative for other writers. She entered her nineties, widowed, blessed with good health, a fine mind, mobility, and energy, but when I urged her to write a memoir, she demurred. She felt she had nothing to say. I kept insisting that she did. (She puts it less gently, saying that I nagged her.) She finally went to the computer and over the course of some four years, wrote, revised, enlarged, revisited her material, and at age ninety-seven, she held her book, *Centennial Memoir: A Tribute to my Parents,* in her hands.

No doubt you have a story about how you came to hold *Memory into Memoir* in your hand. Please consider this book an invitation to pick up the pen. Think of that pen as an oar as you get into your little narrative boat and paddle toward the past.

*April 2021*

# 1 | The Past Meets the Page

*The past is a work of art, free of irrelevancies and loose ends.*
—Comment, Max Beerbohm (1872–1956)

Everyone has memories, but not everyone writes a memoir. Writing a memoir does not pin the past to the page in some sort of static taxidermy; on the contrary, the memoir strives to make the past vivid, available, to make it memorable, for that matter. Writing a memoir returns the writer—and the reader—to those old traditions of storytelling, the sorts of tales once related by elders round ancient campfires, stories rich in lore, a sort of treasury of who we are, how we came to be, and what we owe to our ancestors (even if it's not gratitude). Writing a memoir allows you to endow memory with significance, with structure and voice. Writing a memoir focuses your past, energizes long-lost voices, illuminates anecdote. Writing a memoir means revisiting, reviving family stories. Writing a memoir can be an act of courage or gratitude or a plea for understanding, even a bulwark against loss. Writing a memoir means reconsidering what you thought you already knew. Writing a memoir does not create the past, or even re-create the past, but makes the past legible. Writing a memoir transforms amorphous memory into narrative prose, tangible, a thing with girth and worth. Even a thing of beauty.

The memoir can take many forms, but the question—what is a memoir—might best be answered by what it is not. The memoir cannot boast of being The Truth, but it must certainly aspire to A Truth. The memoir is not a novel, that is to say, fiction, though it uses the same writerly tools. It is neither a legal document, nor an affidavit. It is not the courtroom where the writer testifies under penalty of perjury. However, it is in some fashion, testimony. It's not the confessional that can confer absolution, though certainly there are writers for whom putting the past on paper is itself a victory, and there are writers for whom the pages become a vessel of understanding, if not absolution.

The memoir is different from an autobiography in terms of scope. Autobiography, usually written by an elderly person, suggests the chronological sweep of a whole life, structured from childhood to old age. The memoir is a smaller slice of a person's life. Frank McCourt wrote two more memoirs following *Angela's Ashes*. Dani Shapiro, Mary Karr, Patti Smith, Helen Forrester, Penelope Lively, Rick Bass, and even Tina Turner have all written several memoirs exploring different aspects, and different time periods of their lives. A person might write many memoirs, but only one autobiography.

A memoir usually covers a specific era in the writer's life such as childhood or adolescence. It can concentrate on discrete life events such as parenthood or a divorce, or some other particular moment. One writer I worked with described the summers she spent at a Camp Fire Girls camp in northern California, a work that eventually became a history of that camp published by the Kern County Historical Society. Another writer picked up the pen to describe her experience as a cook on an African entomological expedition fifty years earlier, and her return to an America that was as changed as she was. But the memoir can certainly expand beyond these singular life events. The memoir can explore one's professional life, as does Anthony Bourdain's *Kitchen Confidential*. (And very often you'll find that mini-memoirs serve as the introduction to nonfiction books, a personal account of how the writer came by their passion for their field.) The memoir can also weave together different kinds of experiences. The wildly successful *Eat, Pray, Love* combines exotic travel with the author's pain and confusion over a divorce and a doomed love affair. Travel writing itself can be a form of memoir, observation interwoven with experience and history. In *The Hundred Mile Walk: An Armenian Odyssey*, Dawn Anahid MacKeen tells parallel stories of her grandfather's experience in Turkey in 1915, and her own travels reconstructing his unthinkable journey. Cheryl Strayed in *Wild* combined the challenge of the Pacific Crest Trail with her grief at her mother's death. The memoir can be a portrait of someone who loomed large in the life of the writer, say, a powerful but abusive parent, a beloved but difficult sibling like Norman McLean's *A River Runs Through It*, or a beloved but difficult child like Paula Becker's *A House on Stilts: Mothering in the Age of Opiate Addiction*. The memoir can place a little-known individual at the heart of exciting events. (Everyone who so much as sipped a coffee at a Parisian café in the 1920s seems to have written a memoir.) In some ways, *The Alice B. Toklas Cookbook* is as much a memoir as Ruth Reichl's *Tender at the Bone*.

The memoir can also record stories outside the immediate experience of the author. Vladimir Nabokov's wonderful *Speak, Memory* begins with long, digressive chapters on his maternal and paternal grandparents and their lives and adventures in nineteenth-century Russia, long before the writer was born. Alexander Stille in *The Force of Things: A Marriage in Peace and War* tells the compelling story of his parents' uneasy marriage: his father an Italian Jew escaped from the Fascists, his mother a WASP American princess. The memoir can also tell the story of someone adjacent to one's own life. In *H is for Hawk*, Helen MacDonald melds her hawking experience and her grief at her father's death with a tense inquiry into the life of the writer T. H. White (1906–1964). Martha Oliver-Smith's memoir, *Martha's Mandala*, is rooted in her own childhood and youth, but her real subject is her artistic grandmother, Martha Bacon, who was married to an autocratic poet. (Yes, that seems a strange combination, but it was true.) One of my favorite memoirs, Maxine Kingston's *Woman Warrior*, a series of essays, opens with "No Name Woman," an imaginative reconstruction of an ancestor whose very existence has been erased.

A family memoir can and should enlarge upon events not directly experienced by the writer, particularly if all that might be otherwise lost. Certainly this was true for my mother, Peggy Kalpakian Johnson. Initially she followed one of the prompts given in the next chapter, but in doing so, the thought came to her that she alone could preserve her parents' story. Peggy was the last living person in her immediate family and only she could save their experience from dwindling into threadbare recollection as the years and generations passed.

## The First-Person Narrator

The writer of a memoir will labor under constraints that the novelist does not face. The novelist has the option of creating a narrator distant, quite apart from the characters—a third-person narrator, one in which *all* the characters are "he" or "she." The third-person narrator can easily hop from one person's deepest thoughts to another's. The third-person narrator can observe events from multiple points of view, as in, for instance, *The Grapes of Wrath* where Steinbeck moves the story among various members of the Joad family. The third-person narrator offers the writer and the reader breadth. The memoir, on the other hand, is obliged to be rooted in an "I" through whom the story will pass. This does not mean that "I" must be present in every scene, witness to everything, but "I" is the conduit through which the tale is told. The first-person narrator offers the writer and the reader depth, intimacy. When novelists want to suggest this sort of intimacy, they employ a first-person narrator, an "I," to tell their tales. (Think Nick Carraway in *The Great Gatsby*, Scout Finch in *To Kill a Mockingbird*, as far back as Daniel Defoe's nefarious *Moll Flanders* and the unrepentant *Roxana, the Fortunate Mistress*.) Unlike fiction, the first-person narrator of the memoir has an added, even deeper implied intimacy: *I alone can tell this tale.*

These considerations have corollaries. First among them is that *I lived to tell this tale.* Thus, with a story like Frank McCourt's *Angela's Ashes*, we know that however unthinkable, abysmal, and impoverished was his childhood, he lived through it. We hold his book in our hands. In picking up Cheryl Strayed's *Wild*, we don't know if she conquered the Pacific Crest Trail, but we know she lived through the attempt. We hold her book in our hands. In a novel the central character can die, but the memoir cannot end in the death and destruction of the Narrator. (Unless indeed, like *The Autobiography of Malcolm X*, or Paul Monette's AIDS memoir, *Borrowed Time*, the author himself dies, and the task is finished by someone else.)

Secondly, *I alone can tell this tale* presupposes there *is* a tale. However bizarre the events in the memoir, readers trust that the Narrator is sane, that her tale will be coherent. Novelists are often fond of that wily creature, the Unreliable Narrator, whose story might leap all around in time, in essence, insisting that the reader must run after that story (and insuring that the reader will always arrive a little late and probably out of breath). For the writer of a memoir, to billow off into the incoherent breaks an implied pact with the reader. Though the narrator of a memoir may be inflamed (and the narrative colored) by emotion, and though the story needn't be wholly straightforward, the narrator of a memoir is generally thought to be more reliable than the narrator of fiction.

The memoir is also generally assumed to be a story with *shape*, an arc that suggests a journey from one set of circumstances to another; in short, some sort of change effected. Change can be organic as from childhood to adulthood, or tumultuous as a chronicle of exile, or political, or sexual awareness, or coming through trauma, or a journey to wellness, or travels and adventures, or even a story of someone more beautiful, more doomed, more courageous than the pen-wielding author. Even those books of memoir essays (such as the already mentioned *Woman Warrior* and *Speak, Memory*) true, you could open it to any one essay, read, and be rewarded. But read front to back, the order in which the essays are given, suggests an overall thematic.

The implication in writing a memoir is always that the narrator learned, grew; that the narrator is somehow altered by the events she describes. The most important guide for writer of a memoir is this: *the memoir is not the story of what you know, it is the story of how you learned it.*

————

Why write a memoir? No one's life can be encapsulated by the Sum of Their Posts, the Sum of Their Tweets, those threadlike connections that hover in a disembodied cloud, Why write a memoir? *Because* you alone can tell this tale—even if, like Camp Fire Girls summer camp, or the African entomological expedition, you shared that experience with others. Your story is worth that effort. If you do not convey it to the page, those events, those emotions, those people and places will dwindle and attenuate over time. Those summer days, those frosty nights, that pealing laughter, those tears, that shriek of shock will all dissolve into nothingness. Conversely, I can promise you that once you start to write, the past will open up for you; it will deepen and develop. The more you write your memoir, the more your memories will accrue and accelerate. You will remember what you did not know you had forgotten.

# 2 | In the Beginning?

*"Begin at the beginning,"* the King said, very gravely,
*"and go on till you come to the end: then stop."*
—Lewis Carroll, *Alice's Adventures in Wonderland*, 1865

B eginnings are always difficult, vexing, frustrating. Where to begin? How? Anyone starting a memoir will see roiling before their
eyes a thicket of people, a tangle of events, many befogged, some
befuddled. How to reconstruct the past? Do you as a writer address it
as a series of events, like falling dominos, one event leading inexorably
to another—in other words, how-could-it-be-otherwise? Or as a quilt
that can be ceaselessly ripped up and re-patterned, maybe using the
same squares, but bringing them together under new motifs? Beginnings are messy. Accept that. If you write *Chapter One* and expect the
rest of the story to ribbon out from there, you could end up staring at
those two words, *Chapter One*, for a very long time. Indeed, you could
end up with a sort of writerly paralysis. Start instead with writing that
is simple, declarative, unadorned, and later add depth and detail and
develop narrative from that core; thus, the process of Describe/
Develop/Create.

DESCRIBE: Spark swiftly. Visual/sensory description.
DEVELOP: Expand. Add details. Ask questions of your material.
Even if you don't have answers, the questions are important.
CREATE: Using the details and descriptions, make narrative from
what you have. Put it into scenes, into a story, remembering
that this too is draft and will be enhanced and enriched later
on. The writing doesn't have to be beautiful; it just has to *be*.

Use whatever is at hand to spark your process of Describe, Develop, and Create. Old addresses, photographs, fading Polaroids,

ordinary objects, fleeting sensory recollections—any of these can offer an avenue to turn memory into memoir.

## Prompt: The Object

1. DESCRIBE this object: Every little thing you can recall about it. Not just looks. Smell. Sound. The heft or texture. Make your information detailed and complex. Good grammar not essential!

2. DEVELOP: Put this object *into a context*. How do you see it and where? Describe vividly not just the object, but its *environment*, indeed its ambience (which will require memory and imagination). *The context will affect the object.* For instance:

   Is the prom dress on the sewing machine or on the dance floor? (That is, the difference between the prom dress laying across the sewing machine still in pieces, or being waltzed around the decorated gym with a corsage pinned to it.)

   Is the upright piano in your living room or in the tavern on 4th and Grand?

   Is the frying pan on the stove or is it in the back of the van, ready for a camping trip?

   Is the chemistry set in the garage or classroom?

   The doll in the arms of a child has a different context, time frame, and ambience than a doll languishing at the bottom of a closet.

   The sleeping bag rolled out on the bare springs of a youth hostel bed among snoring, foreign strangers has a different ambience than the one you took to pajama parties as a kid.

3. CREATE a scene using the context you have developed in which you *ally this object to an individual*. Are you the one pushing the lawn mower? Who is playing the flute and where: a recital, a marching band, alone on the front porch, a summer night? The scene should not only describe the physical world, but also evoke the *mood as-*

*sociated* with this object. Moreover, the *individual* allied to this object should be as clearly drawn as the object itself.

———

But perhaps the past is not available to you in solid, reliable objects, nouns. Perhaps you can only remember it in shards.

## *Prompt: First Things Fast*

FIRST SOUND: Do you have an early recollection of a persistent or particular sound? (Traffic? Thunder? The ice-cream truck? Gears grinding? A doorbell? Thumping of a rolling pin? Typewriter? Radio or television voices, theme songs or ad ditties? Rain?)

FIRST SCENT: Is there a scent or an odor or an aroma that zaps you right back to . . . maybe you are not even sure where it takes you. Cooking scents? Seasonal scents? Exhaust? Manure? Paint?

FIRST SONG: What is the first song you remember? Who sang it? Can you sing it? Even in bits?

FIRST TV SHOW: Can you still hum or sing the theme song? Hear the voices? Remember bits or episodes?

FIRST MEMORABLE TEACHER: Portrait? How/where do you see them? Name?

FIRST FRIEND: Does this friend have a context? Home? School? Name? Description?

FIRST BED OR BEDROOM you remember sleeping in, or waking in.

FIRST PET: Name? Description? In what context do you see this critter? What happened to this pet?

FIRST CAR AND/OR PUBLIC TRANSPORT: Color? Make? Year? Where do you see this vehicle? And/or where is the stop where you got on or off this public transport?

FIRST JOURNEY of your recollection? Where? Circumstances?

FIRST "EMERGENCY": Wind? Rain? Fire? Earthquake? Someone suddenly ill?

FIRST TIME YOU RECOGNIZED THAT someone important had left this world. (Doesn't have to be a relative or friend; could be Kurt Cobain or Elvis, or a pet for that matter.) Where were you?

If you have more than one "first" for each, fine. Do not corset yourself into correctness. If some of these memories are yours by way of photographs, or family stories, fine. Let these First/Fast descriptions roll around in your mind for a bit—like billiard balls clacking into one another—and return to them to develop. Combine those that are linked.

Let's look at the First choices of a writer named Genetta (Netta) Gibbs Swanson. Netta was the youngest of four children; the eldest, Joe, was about fourteen years her senior. As a little child Netta spent a lot of time with her deeply religious Granny who lived with the family. Whatever else Netta had amid her First Things, these three are chronologically linked, and combined they will create narrative.

FIRST SONG: Amazing Grace
FIRST SCENT(s): shoe polish and aftershave (or possibly men's hair gel)
FIRST TV SHOW: unspecified televangelist programs

### SATURDAY NIGHT AND SUNDAY MORNING

My grandmother came to live with us after Grandpa died. Our house was small, and we were already crowded. Granny got her own room, and in return, she also got all the housework. Granny was a devoutly religious woman. Her life had been spent financially pinched and emotionally denied, so I honestly think religion gave her an outlet, a release, a chance to shout and sing. Since I was the youngest, about three or four at the time, I was at home while Gary and Delia went to school and Daddy and Mama worked. After they all left the house in the mornings, the television would go on, and Granny would set up the ironing board in front of it, and she and

I would be shouting and singing along with the televangelist, and the choir, and all the people being saved. If she was working in the kitchen, we just turned the TV up really loud. Granny and I got saved daily. The rest of the world then might have been belting out "Dancing Queen," but it's "Amazing Grace" I remember and that can still make me misty. I knew every verse of "Amazing Grace" at the age of four, and I had a fine, strong singing voice, even then, so everyone at church thought I was a holy prodigy. Granny and I got to jump and shout at church too. Only she and I went to church. Everyone else slept in on Sundays. But once my brother Joe came home, Sunday mornings changed.

I had been told that Joe was coming home after eighteen months in the army. Fort Dix, my mother said. Actually (I later learned) Joe was in prison for Grand Theft Auto. My family was less interested in deluding me with this little lie, than in deluding themselves and the neighbors. Joe must have been about 20 or 21 when he came home from the pen. It wasn't enough for Granny that he had paid his debt to society, so to speak, but he must be saved. She was all over Joe to give himself up to the Lord. Night and day, she wouldn't let it rest. She'd mark passages in the Bible and leave them at his place at the table, or under his pillow! Now and then she might go after my other brother, Gary, or my sister, Delia, occasionally my parents, but Joe's soul was her Cross.

Joe had a job working for Bennie Kaufman's dad at Kaufman's TV and Appliances. Bennie was his best friend from high school. Joe worked evenings there so Bennie's dad could be home with the family. Joe didn't mind.

On Saturday nights, Joe always went out. We had one bathroom and after he was done showering and getting ready, I would walk in there and smell the glamour, the scent of Going Out. Aftershave and men's hair gel, of soap and maybe deodorant for all I know. In the back porch, Joe would polish his shoes, Shinola on the brush, back and forth, enough rhythm to make me want to dance while I watched him. Granny didn't bother him in the bathroom, but the back porch wasn't safe, and she'd still hound him about bad companions and not being saved. Joe hardly ever spoke. I guess prison cured him of that, but he never sassed Granny either. He knew better. He was always real calm. Maybe he learned that in prison too. And when he left on Saturday night, he always said Goodnight Granny, Goodnight Nettaspeck. He called me that because I was so small.

He came back home early on Sunday mornings when Granny and I were getting ready for church. Someone would let him off— we heard the car in the alley, but we never did see who it was. He'd come through the back door, tousled and disheveled, tired, a stubble on his chin, and his clothes all rumpled. He'd greet us like he was happy to see us, and ask Granny if he'd missed breakfast. Even on Sunday morning, Joe smelled like Saturday night, Glamour and Going Out. Of shoe polish and hair gel and aftershave, cigarettes and maybe a whiff of a girl's cologne. Between Saturday night's aftershave and Sunday morning's "Amazing Grace," I knew, sensed somehow there was a huge divide.

Granny couldn't resist the chance to rattle on at Joe about being saved, and the like, but she wasn't a woman to sit still, so she'd have to be up and cooking. Joe would eat and listen, sometimes ask for more, and when Granny's back was turned, he'd wink at me, like he and I, angel and devil, youngest and oldest, were somehow united against all the rest of them, the whole family. The whole town for that matter. Maybe the whole world.

––––

In connecting three Firsts, Netta has expanded all of them. "Saturday Night and Sunday Morning" is short, less than a thousand words, evocative, but much in need of some revising and refining, and expanding. Her narrative wanders here and there (the bits about Bennie and the appliance store could use some edits) and the paragraphing and transitions aren't always great. Visuals on Granny and Joe would be a nice addition. But this memoir essay has rich material Netta can continue to mine and build on. As she revises (say, adding dialogue and scenic depiction, for instance) it will open up, become an actual chapter.

Notice her title. Having a title even from the beginning is a good writerly practice. A title is a buoy, not an anchor. A title will help you focus your material. However, titles are fluid, and if your focus changes (and it probably will), then change the title. "Saturday Night and Sunday Morning" suits Netta's story, but it's not the only possible title (though it's certainly better than her original choice, "Granny and Me"). "Saturday Night and Sunday Morning" includes Joe without having to name him. When you change the title, you also alter what you are telegraphing to the reader about significance. F. Scott Fitzgerald's original title for *The Great Gatsby* was *Trilmachio in West Egg*. Think on that!

First Things Fast can also be expanded beyond the realm of childhood.

FIRST JOB you ever had: Where? Coworkers? Wage? Duties? Bosses? Does that job still exist?

FIRST BOYFRIEND/GIRLFRIEND or crush.

FIRST CAR of your own. Make, model, color, anything else . . .

FIRST APARTMENT OR DORM ROOM: Your roommate was . . .

FIRST PROFESSIONAL JOB: Workplace, duties, co-workers, bosses? Does this job still exist?

FIRST TIME you thought you might actually fail at something.

FIRST TIME you thought you might actually succeed at something.

FIRST MEETING with the person who became a spouse, longtime partner, or dear friend.

Beyond Firsts, you can use Describe/Develop/Create with other memories: the four places or times you were happiest. The four places or times you were the most beset with anxiety. The goal is to create material that you can then shape and structure.

## Prompt: Writing from Photographs

Perhaps some of your Firsts are not actual memories, but what you have absorbed from old photos, perhaps even photos taken before you were born. Bringing Describe/Develop/Create to photographs can often fill out, inform, where actual memory cannot quite go.

Go back through your old photos and find a few that "speak" to you.

1. DESCRIBE THE SNAPSHOT: Short, succinct notes. Who is in this photo? What is the background? Where was it taken? When? What are they wearing?

2. DEVELOP THE SNAPSHOT: Ask questions of the photo. Is it associated with some occasion or incident? Does it have a mood that you can either identify or imagine? Is there evidence anywhere of the relationships of the people in the photo? Not simply familial or friendship, but perhaps how they felt about one another, or their emotions at the time. Does their stance or posture suggest certain circumstances? Search the photo for evidence of the season, the weather, the time of day. If the photo is in black and white, color it as best you can. What about what we *can't* see? For instance, who is taking the photo? What is just beyond or behind or nearby the objects in the photo? Can you put *sounds* in the photo? (Music, wind, background conversation?) Can you add to it some physical sensation, such as scent, remembered or imagined?

3. CREATE A SCENE BUILDING ON THESE ELEMENTS: Though a photo is static, put these people in motion, perhaps just before or just after the shutter snaps on them.

Here is the photo Netta Gibbs used, and what she makes of it. She isn't concerned with getting glorious prose on the page, nor even much with following correct grammatical style; the goal here is to note the short, the sharp, the observant.

1. DESCRIPTION: Family in the backyard standing beside the old Chevy. Clothesline in the background. Me, aged 3, Mother, Dad,

Delia age 10, Gary age 13, Joe age 18, Granny, ancient. Everyone in Sunday best. Granny holding her Bible, me with my stiff-petticoat dress. Dandelions in the little patch of grass, so . . . spring. People squint against the sunshine. Shadows say it's morning. Black Chevy sedan we had for eons. I judge this photo to be about 1977. Granny came to live with us after Gramps' death in 1976.

2. DEVELOP: Why was this taken in the backyard? Mama was a front porch kind of girl. Few people ever got to see our backyard which was nothing but a scrap of lawn, a clothesline and tool shed. But here it is immortalized forever, the clothesline complete with clothes flapping on it—including my father's boxer shorts! Why would my mother allow such a picture to be taken? I alone look happy, but then I loved my Mary Janes and that dress. It was pink and made of some stiff fabric, or maybe that's just because Granny starched everything. But everyone else looks . . . well, certainly NOT happy. My father has that tense, terse, worried expression I later came to know as default for him. He looks to be in pain, but this was long before he got sick. My mother is staring straight ahead, like she's having a mug shot and not a family photo. My brother Gary looks smug and snotty. Delia's bored. Joe's eyes look vacant. Granny is holding Joe's arm like he might run away. I can all but feel Granny quake as I look at the picture. But quake with what? Rage? Fear? Joe and my father are wearing white shirts and ties, and suit jackets. The whole picture has an expectant feel to it, like we were *going* somewhere, not coming home. But where are we going? We hardly ever went anywhere, the whole family. Anyway, that many people couldn't all fit in that car at once.

Donna! Donna took the picture! Joe's girlfriend, Donna! Donna was with him in the stolen car. He stole the car, and picked Donna up. He took her joyriding for the rest of the day, until that night when the cops pulled him over for speeding, and arrested him for theft. He said Donna had nothing to do with it. It was all his idea. They let Joe out on bail (God only knows what my dad used for money for his bond) but he had to go back to court for trial. I'll bet this was that day. My parents knew we won't all be together again for a long time. In this picture my brother Gary revels in my parents' pain (as he did for thirty years). My grandmother is mad at the devil for having tempted Joe, and mad at Joe for having succumbed. Joe, I can't altogether read his expression, half-ashamed, half-unrepentant. I know though that for the whole 18 months my mother maintained to the neighbors and everyone else that he had joined the army, and was stationed at Fort Dix.

Netta roams all over, forward and backward in time, filling in the photo with context and backgrounds, with emotions. The scene Netta can create from what she has written is the salient fact that this photo was not an occasion the Gibbs family would want others to witness. That's why they were in the backyard, and why Mom didn't even care that underwear flapped on the clothesline. This photograph was, in its way, a sadly momentous, private occasion.

## HISTORICAL PHOTOGRAPHS

The advent of photography in the mid-nineteenth century has given us windows to the past. Who can forget those Matthew Brady photographs from the Civil War? One hundred and fifty years later, they still shock. Many families have old photos that freeze-in-frame not just occasions, but emotionally revealing moments, especially for people who were too unsophisticated to guard their expressions. In her *Centennial Memoir*, Peggy Kalpakian Johnson used many historic family photos to great effect. To me the most heartbreaking of these is a studio photograph taken in 1908 in Adana, a city in southeastern Turkey where Peggy's mother, Haigouhi, lived until 1921. In the picture a mother and her daughter stand stiffly, side by side. The daughter (Haigouhi's older sister) was about to emigrate, and you can tell from their eyes that mother and daughter both know they will never see each other again—and they never did. Clearly, they had two copies made. The daughter brought one with her to America (which is how it survived). The other, so we were told, was buried, along with all the other family photographs, so that the Turks should never find them when they invaded the house in 1915.

Pictures and videos snapped on smartphones are now so ubiquitous that it's hard to remember that a camera was often a gift to honor a special occasion. For my sixth grade graduation my parents gave me a Brownie, one of those little black boxes where with a single click I could photograph my best friends in black and white. When glorious Kodachrome came into being, color seemed to *pop!* off the picture. No one knew then that these colors would all fade to yellow, or that the once highly prized Polaroid photos would grow wholly gray and blurry. Even so, these photos can be truly fruitful for the writer.

In asking questions of the past, even the past frozen, static in a photograph, you can stir memory's metaphorical pot and breathe in its fumes.

## Prompt: The Overview

Renata Pierce often amused her friends with stories of her travels with her restless, globe-trotting mother, Sylvia. But when she went to write a memoir about this complex woman, she had trouble balancing the madcap and amusing with the poignant, possibly tragic. Renata also found herself stymied by the implied cast of thousands (concierges, flight attendants, assorted drivers, tutors, tour guides, pickpockets, gendarmes, etc.) who were extras in her life. Seeking a narrative path through this welter of possibility, she created an Overview by responding to some general questions, filling in details, amplifying on the meaning of her answers.

WHEN was this person (or persons) born? Siblings?
WHERE did they live in their youth?
A Bronx walk-up? A Nebraska farm? Rural Idaho? Sprawling Houston, or greater Miami? Bring in any details available to you, even if you know them only through hearsay.

WHERE did they go to school?

One-room schoolhouse? Catholic school? Large inner-city school? Segregated schools? Home-schooled? If they went to college, was it a sprawling state university? A small, prim, private college? Schooling can include training or apprenticeship or military service.

WHICH historical events impacted their lives?

Any war will significantly impact lives far beyond the soldiers who fought in it. Indeed, those who were too young to remember, those born after will often grow up in a world altered by that war, new political realities like those following the Civil War, or the Cold War following the end of World War II. When Americans pulled out of Vietnam, refugees from Southeast Asia flooded into American life, and the children were thrust into American schools. Vast economic reversals like the Great Depression, or the COVID-19 pandemic, and all their social upheavals affect the lives of adults and children alike. Social migrations like the Great Migration from the South into cities of the north in the early years of the twentieth century meant that people had to forge new traditions. The Civil Rights era impacted lives both Black and white. Cultural moments like the late 1960s, or the McCarthy era, shaped lives and core beliefs for decades. Weather disasters like Hurricane Katrina, Hurricane Maria, and climate change, and catastrophes like long droughts and wildfires, alter lives, push people to uproot or rebuild.

WHAT (if any) personal upheavals affected their lives?

Loss of a parent? Chronic or debilitating illness? Drug abuse? Alcohol? Industrial accident? Divorce? Job loss?

WHEN did they marry? Whom? Married how many times? Divorced? Widowed? Children?

JOBS/PROFESSIONS?

PASSIONS/SKILLS/CHARACTER TRAITS that affected their lives?

My late mother, Sylvia, was the most restless person on earth. Life with her was never dull. She could domesticate an airport bathroom, or charm a gendarme, but poor you, if you could not keep up with her. And none of us could. She was always in transit. Even at the end. She died of Covid 19 on a cruise ship far away from any of us. And maybe she was all right with that. I'll never know. Travel to her was like a drug, something she could not resist. (She had nothing but contempt for other sorts of drugs as my brother learned to his sorrow.)

She grew up in Astoria, Oregon. (Maybe her proximity to the sea, the Oregon coast, was a factor in her life-long restlessness.) She was always very coy about her age, but she was born in 1935. Her father was a commercial fisherman and she hated that he smelled of fish and cigarettes. Her mother was schoolteacher, who smelled of chalk dust and dandruff which Sylvia also hated. She was the third of five children which meant, as she informed us on many occasions, that she never wore anything that wasn't hand-me-down. Sylvia, by contrast, more or less created herself. Sylvia was self-consciously elegant in all things, the way she dressed, the way she smoked, the way she held a glass. She made a wicked martini, and was known to drink to excess. Sometimes frequently.

Sylvia graduated from Astoria High School in about 1953, but I have never seen a yearbook, or anything to connect her to Astoria after she left and became what was quaintly known as a stewardess. She began with some lackluster, long-vanished airline, moving up to Pan Am (not lackluster, but certainly long vanished). Being a stewardess was a glamorous occupation in the 50's and '60's, and her job certainly fed, maybe even satisfied her passion for travel at least for a while. But when I see those photographs of her and the other stewardesses in their svelte uniforms waving gaily on the tarmac, I have to wonder how she learned to walk up and down the narrow aisles in high heels and a tight skirt and a big gleaming smile plastered across her face no matter what.

Not surprisingly she met my dad Maxwell Pierce on an intercontinental flight in First Class. (She wouldn't have given some poor dude in economy a refill on his Coke). Max's father invented the shopping cart. The patent on this invention—stupidly commonplace as it is—made gizillions. Max was the only child of the inventor's second wife, and she was many years younger than the old man. Max grew up on a ten acre estate near Honolulu with a vast view of the Pacific, with servants for everything, and, so it seemed to me, very little in the way of affection from either parent. He was older than Sylvia by maybe eight years. He had been married before, but had no children. She swept him off his feet.

Sylvia and Maxwell Pierce had three children, two girls and a boy. I am the second daughter. We lived in Montecito, near Santa Barbara, and even more posh than Santa Barbara, and went to private schools. When my grandmother died, we moved to the ten acre estate in Hawaii, and went to private school there, Punahou. But mostly we traveled. First class of course. I saw York before I saw New York. I rode a camel in Cairo before I rode a bicycle. I learned to ski in Gstadd, Switzerland.

But my father did not have a mania for travel. He didn't have a mania for anything, or any real ambition. He was more of a collector, a dilettante, who dabbled in real estate and stocks and stuff like that. They divorced when I was about 14. My older sister had just started college. My brother and I went with mom.

Max must have been generous with Sylvia in the divorce settlement because our traveling did not slow down one bit. In fact, without my father to demur or protest, we were on the go more than ever. Sylvia signed us up to travel with some Arabs in Jordan, to camp with them in their tents. On safari I ate roasted ants in Africa with barefoot natives. I saw Carnival first-hand in Rio. All of which left me terrified. We were traveling so much she engaged private tutors for me and my brother. The tutors were always young men. Some were more memorable than others. (Note to self: Sebastian.)

If I tell the story chronologically, the early parts won't indicate her energy and zest, or her unflinching egotism. So . . . what if I write up a few memorable incidents? Maybe I'll begin with the ones where I was terrified, where she shone for me. Or where she failed me. I'll bring in the backgrounds slowly, sprinkling the info where it's needed. The best way to portray her is through her singular passion, travel, which sometimes I think she was running from as much as she was traveling to. Running from what?

Notice Renata does not build her Overview using the questions in the order they were asked. Reshuffle your narrative deck however suits your material. Her Overview has keyed in elements of a strategy to get this complex story (and this complex woman) on the page. The process has also suggested those elements the writer can diminish. Chronology alone will not serve this writer; Renata will not begin, a la *David Copperfield*, with "I am born." She'll start with those places/ incidents where Sylvia was most vivid to her daughter, the narrator. Writing these up singly, Renata can revise later and decide then how to structure them to make a whole.

## Prompt: Lists

However simple, chronology can sometimes offer an avenue into writing your memoir. You can use Describe/Develop/Create as a technique with boating expeditions, sporting competitions, motorcycles you have known, mountains you have climbed, countries you have traveled to, rodeos or horses you have ridden, gardens you have reveled in or wrestled with, foster homes, feasts; in short, any important, repeatable element of your past. This is basically what Raymond Carver did with his wonderful poem, "The Car." Each line starts out "The car that . . ." and goes on to itemize, swiftly, something about all his different cars. Sometimes it's something ordinarily mechanical, but some lines chronicle important events, dire events like drunk driving, or humorous ones like getting laid. This is not narrative prose, but each short, pithy line is full of promise for a memoir.

Addresses are an especially useful way to approach the past. Not everyone can list their rodeos, but everyone has had addresses, some more memorable than others. My mother, who initially resisted my suggestion of writing a memoir, only reluctantly began listing the addresses where she had lived as a child. She started with 905 Harding Avenue, Venice, California. Peggy, born 1922 in Constantinople, was a toddler when her parents, Haroutune and Haigouhi Kalpakian, immigrated to America in 1923. Peggy had no recollection of the journey, but she certainly remembered this ten room, two-storied house with a high turret, and a broad wrap-around porch. This gracious home must have seemed palatial to immigrants who had just traveled second-class from Greece. The house belonged to Peggy's aunt and uncle. (The aunt was the girl in the 1908 photograph; the uncle was a well-to-do Santa Monica pharmacist who had signed the documents sponsoring the Kalpakians' immigration.) Peggy, her parents, and her older sister did not live in glamorous 905 Harding, but rather in the two-room gardener's cottage on the sprawling property. Four years later they moved to a one-bedroom house on a canal in Venice and thence to an apartment on Alberta Street, quarters behind a grocery shop my grandfather rented and where he worked. In all, between 1923 and 1940, the Kalpakians had six addresses in Los Angeles.

Writing about each address opened for Peggy a door to the past. Describing and Developing, around each house there came to cluster anecdotes, some of which she hadn't thought of in years, many of which she had never shared with us. One of my favorites is the story of how the three Kalpakian daughters created their own "radio." They hid in a big cardboard box in the living room and offered up "radio programs" for their parents' delight and applause. They didn't have a radio, but they knew how it worked. As the pages of addresses grew, my mother realized her parents' story was much larger than mere addresses, and that's when she began a new folder on her computer, *CENTENNIAL MEMOIR*, so named because her parents had married in 1917, a hundred years before.

## The "Set Piece"

Perhaps, quite apart from any of these suggestions, you have a vivid, compelling scene from your past that, for whatever reason, begs to be written. That, too, is a good place to start. In putting this scene on the page do not, at this point, worry about what might come before, or what might come after, or how it will be connected to the whole. All those considerations will work themselves out. As you create material and revise, you'll come to understand the, shall we say, tendons and ligaments necessary to connect it to the rest. Pick up the pen, and put this inspiring scene on the page. You'll find that such inspiration is contagious and can light up other episodes and chapters.

———

Writing is a process more on the order of making bread than of making a cocktail where, a jigger of this, a splash of that, a little garnish, and *Voila! Drink up!* With bread, you measure your yeast and flour, stir, create a ball, leave it, come back, punch down, knead again, then shape—all this *before* you bake. Approach your memoir in this patient mode: stirring, adding, leavening, shaping. Remember that draft is endlessly flexible, and anything not in actual print with an ISBN number is draft. In the writing process, save whatever you cut in a separate file because probably you can use it elsewhere. Using Describe/Develop/Create on the raw materials of your past, you will find that scenes and details will accrue, combine, enlarge, entwine with one another. Fashion these into memoir essays to begin with; do not, at this point, fret what order they might go in, or even quite how they might relate to one another. You can combine and condense and reorder later when you come to revisions. For now, create as much draft as you can.

The more you write, the more the past will come to you, not whole cloth (there is no whole cloth of the past; there never was), but in bits and scraps, and you will use imagination to hem, connect, fuse, finesse, to put pattern over what might otherwise look to be merely a chaotic jumble of events. A false start is better than no start.

# 3 | Lost Domains

*And the rocket's red glare, the bombs bursting in air,*
*gave proof through the night that our flag was still there!*
—Francis Scott Key (1814)

Transforming private memory into narrative memoir requires landscapes, whether of great vistas like homesteading in Alaska, or gritty city streets, or domestic interiors, scenes from the past that are, that have become, lost domains Some are lost to disaster like pre-Katrina New Orleans or lower Manhattan, pre-9/11. Some are lost to tides or building codes or zoning regulations or defunct industries. Fields of once-wavy alfalfa that are now rigid parallel streets of tract houses. A gentrified condominium was once an apartment block where kids played stickball at dusk and, at least in memory, no one locked their doors. Some lost domains are eroded by mere time, a job that simply no longer exists, or a wringer washing machine and the squeal of a clothesline on pulleys. Lost domains can also be ritual tamale-making at Christmastime, or making raspberry jam in the summer, the creak of oars in boats on summer mornings.

In the memoir, these lost domains must be conveyed scenically. To make their scenes vivid, prose writers labor under narrative obligations that the lucky screenwriter can easily sidestep. The screenwriter puts on the page *Exterior. Night. Rainy alley lit by a single bulb* and trots right along, relying on the set decorator, the lighting person, the prop person, the sound designer to bring the scene to life. You, dear writer, are on your own. The responsibility for creating, or rather re-creating, these landscapes rests with the author. Narrative prose moves forward by describing events and characters scenically and by moving characters through scenes. If those scenes are not vividly depicted, the characters—their emotions, their motives, their actions—float and bob, untethered in a sea of words.

You, the writer, might very well picture—see in your mind's eye—the scene implicit in a phrase, such as: "We went home." "We went up on deck." "We ate in the kitchen." "We had an old car." "I was a waitress at a diner." But I, the reader, do not. Put thus they are neither scenic nor descriptive. To transform memory into memoir, each of these generalities begs to be amplified. There's so much missing! The light, the noise, scents and sensory considerations, the weather, comforts or discomforts. How did you get home? What was the road like? Walking? Riding bikes? The feel of the deck beneath your feet, the rolling sensation of a choppy sea? What is the ambience of the kitchen? Is it a stainless-steel wonder? A cramped galley? A place with buckled linoleum, a rust-stained sink, and dead flies on the windowsills?

To make these lost domains vivid for the reader, the writer must not simply note, nor describe: the writer must *evoke*. In doing so, imagine yourself compositely as the set decorator, the lighting person, the prop person, the sound designer, each of whom has the responsibility to create scenic authenticity. Think about how, in all those capacities, you can create conviction on the page using sensory inventory.

## Light

The light by which you illuminate your scenes and characters contributes to the reader's understanding of what these scenes meant in your characters' lives and the life of the author. Light is variable. A single candle can illuminate the darkness, or make fearful and trembling shadows just beyond. The full light of a noonday sun can bathe a whole scene in splendor, or act as a kind of weapon, blinding everyone with its glare. Light is crucial, and varied: fluorescent light, moonlight, lamplight, sunshine, the veil of rain, the glare of neon, light thickened with smoke, light shimmering up from a desert highway, blinding off of snow at midday, the flash from a single bolt of lightning momentarily making plain what otherwise lay in darkness. The rocket's red glare.

"The Star-Spangled Banner" (which began life as a poem) is not a memoir, but it certainly commemorates a salient, dramatic moment in the life of Francis Scott Key. During the War of 1812, the Battle of Baltimore, he and another man were sent as envoys to deal with the British about a prisoner exchange. They were held on a British ship throughout the battle, and from there they watched the nighttime bombardment of Fort McHenry by British guns. In that first stanza the lyrics are full of light, light, light. Key moves light through time, and time through light. "O say can you see by the *dawn's early light* what so proudly we hailed at the *twilight's last gleaming . . .*" (the day before). Then, through the dark, smoky night when lit only by "*the rocket's red glare, the bombs bursting in air*" (italics mine), he could briefly see that the American flag over Fort McHenry still stood, and his heart filled with joy. Without the light, the scene is invisible.

## Soundscapes

Page one of her memoir, *The Heart to Artemis*, the writer Bryher (1894–1983) recounts waking one morning in Lahore, India, wondering why the sounds outside her window, the clatter of the tongas in the street below, were somehow so familiar, even comforting in their way. She realizes that the *clip-clop* sound of hooves had thrust her back vividly to her childhood in late-Victorian London a half-century earlier. In her childhood there were no motorcars (as they were called), no taxis, no airplanes overhead. Apart from distant trains, Bryher's childhood world moved to the sound of hooves, horse-drawn rhythms: smart carriages on the roadways, hansom cabs in the city, horse-drawn omnibuses, enormous workhorses pulling wagons full of goods, and all the attendant noises and voices surrounding.

Noises and voices! Imagine the sounds that informed your past, sounds now vanished. The clack of the typewriter (remembering too that the manual machine had a very different sound than the

IBM Selectric). Even, more recently, the mechanical noise as the CD player moved from one disc to another on random. Maybe you had milk delivered and the clank of the bottles lingers in memory. A long-vanished sound from my own childhood was the tootle of the Helms Bakery truck that plied the streets of full of tract houses in the San Fernando Valley, stopping every now and then to sell bread and sweets to people who would congregate on the street upon hearing the sound of his whistle.

As the sound designer of your memoir, think about the quality of the sounds you want to incorporate and how they affect the timbre of your scene, whether the erratic, annoying, incessant barking of a nearby dog, or the thud of hail, or the crunch of snow underfoot. Sometimes in moments of crisis people will hone their concentration down to a single sound, the drip of a faucet, the tick of a clock—isolated, otherwise inconsequential sounds that can ring with menace or fear or anxiety. Sound creates rhythms. Rhythms can be used on the page to heighten emotions, to enliven scenes that without sound design are static. Think of the diner where once you might have waited tables: call-and-response between the waiter and the line cook, the slap of dirty dishes into buckets as they get bussed back to the sink, the chugging dishwasher, the hiss of the overhead spray, right down to the cracking of eggs and the tumble of ice cubes. Take these things away and you have an Edward Hopper painting: silent, static, mute.

## Prompt: Sensory Information and Scenic Depiction

Have a look through any of your materials from Describe/Develop/Create and select. Save your original piece in a separate folder, and then revise it to expand with scenic detail. Linger. Expand. Invoke.

To begin, you should just splash your impressions on the page. Invoke not merely the props, the visuals, but sensory elements, sound (the hum of an old fridge, the clacking of typewriter keys, and clanging bells in a long-ago office), textures (the sticky feel of the oilcloth in summer), smell (cigarette butts and spent matches), the light. Don't forget present but unseen ambience. A baseball field ought to reek of summer and the sweat of kids playing. A job in retail ought to include the cash register's ping, but also your aching feet, and the smile pasted across your mug. A job waitressing ought to include the awful slurp of vats of ketchup and mayo and relish being turned into Thousand Island dressing. Develop your characters, settings, and environments with details. Vivacity lies with the particulars. Generalities are boring.

Once you've created your sensory inventory, populate your scene. Start another new folder and incorporate what you've done into the original. Weave in the sensory as you move your characters through the landscape, whatever that landscape might be.

A writer in one of my classes, a lifelong educator, wrote about how anxious she had been when she began her first teaching job. In paragraph one she described the classroom, but as a mere list, static, unmoving, dull. In the rewrite she placed her narrator there at the door on that first morning and *walked her through the classroom*, the rows of student desks, the art corner, the bookshelves; thus she was able to imbue these objects not only with better scenic depiction, but with the narrator's emotions about her new job. This lost domain came to life, as did the Narrator's feelings.

One such lost domain for my family is movie theatres, many now succumbed to corporate takeovers and the perils of digital streaming. I wrote the below description of some local theatres as part of a short blogpost on my website in 2019.

DARKENED THEATRES

I brought my kids up with a passion for pictures. I took them to the movies before they weighed enough to hold the seat down. While they were growing up, there were three theatres in this town. In each you immediately entered an enclosed space from which all natural light was banished. Other than that, they had significant differences.

Sunset Square had four small, stuffy auditoriums where your

feet stuck to the spilled pop and popcorn on floor, and the seats were sprung. On summer afternoons mothers would often bring their kids, shoo them to the front, then sit in the back and chat the whole time. The Sehome theatre was where the artsy pictures showed, the Jane Austen remakes. The seats were sprung, but the air was not as bad. The mall had a complex of six theatres, and this was where you went for the Great Big Pictures. The mall theatres were stuffy, but at least they didn't smell, and sprung seats were replaced now and then. However, thunderous artillery from the war film in the next theatre would rattle your fillings in your teeth while on your screen a tender love scene unfolded. Crash! Bang! Boom!

Now, all of these theatres are closed. The mall complex is gone entirely, turned into a chain restaurant. The other two are hulking spaces, shuttered, grim, forlorn. Now, built in what was once a meadow is a new Super Duper Regal complex (sixteen or so auditoriums complete with 3-D and other mega-wonders). Entering this vast, enclosed lobby, you instantly squint against the onslaught of neon and flashing lights. At the concession stands, people mill in long lines like they're awaiting a TSA search. Soft drinks come in the size of horse troughs, popcorn in the equivalent of oaken barrels. The plush seats are so steeply tiered I get vertigo near the top.

A few months later my eldest son, Bear McCreary, wrote a post on his website on very much the same topic (theatres we had loved that are no longer extant). The narrator here *places himself* in these locations, this theatre, this video store; in short, he *inhabits* these scenes. My piece is descriptive, but it lacks emotion. In moving his narrator through the landscape, Bear captures the excitement of his youth, of what these places meant.

## CINEMATIC SHRINES OF MY YOUTH

Unbeknown to me and my high school friends in the mid-1990s, we lived in the twilight of the analog era. In just a few short years the popularization of the Internet would redefine nearly every aspect of our daily lives. But at that time, the most important place in my youth was Crazy Mike's Video at the Sunset Square shopping center.

Every weekend, my family rented armfuls of movies, laying the groundwork for the forty-eight hours ahead. Every employee there knew me, and I knew them. I often called them relentlessly on summer days, wanting to know when a new release was finally out on the shelf. They eventually set titles aside for me, even before I called, just so I would stop pestering them. I pleaded with them to give me their large movie displays and unneeded posters, many of which still adorn the walls of my old room to this day.

In my youth, the analog era, discussion of movies moved at a glacial pace, only via word of mouth. There was no Rotten Tomatoes score to dictate a film's worth in a matter of seconds. Wandering the aisles of Crazy Mike's, my friends and I had only a film's poster and title, and our instincts, to make our choices. The risk of finding a bad movie was part of the allure. Sometimes "bad" movies produced the most memorable evenings. Inspired by intriguing vhx box art, I discovered my favorite cult films, including *Mission in Action 2: The Beginning, Deathstalker II, Moron Movies,* and *American Cyborg: Steel Warrior.* Hidden gems such as *Evil Dead, Dead Alive,* or *Cannibal: The Musical!* made Sam Raimi, Peter Jackson, Trey Parker, and Matt Stone household names in my youth long before their breakout mainstream hits like *Spider-Man, Lord of the Rings,* and *South Park,* respectively.

The Sunset Square Mall also housed one of the city's two multiplexes, Sunset Square Cinema. I saw an unfathomable number of films there over the years, in an admittedly pretty terrible theater. There was practically no sound insulation at all, so every film had a constant low-end rumble permeating the soundtrack, explosions from neighboring films. But I loved it nonetheless.

I saw *The Shadow* three nights in a row at this theater. Only on the third consecutive viewing did I realize I actually didn't care for the movie and that I was simply returning to experience Jerry Goldsmith's gothic score. When *Braveheart* returned to theaters in February of 1996, I saw it here for what would be my seventh theatrical viewing, and I bawled my eyes out at the end with my entire family and the one other audience member, a big jock guy who was seated a few rows in front of us. The last film I recall seeing at Sunset Square was *South Park: Bigger, Longer & Uncut*, where I nearly died of laughter-induced convulsions during the "Uncle Fucker" number.

The Sunset Square cinema has since been gutted and turned into a Goodwill. Though the entrance is sealed off, its marquee is still in place, a sad reminder of what used to be.

## Scenic Depiction to Move Characters through Time

Shortly after college, I was very briefly a social worker, not an experience worthy of a memoir, but it returned to me vividly when I wrote *Graced Land*. The central figure, Emily Shaw, is (not surprisingly) a bookish recent college grad unsuited to her job as a social worker in St. Elmo, California. In chapter two, after calling on welfare recipient and passionate Elvis fan, Joyce Jackson, Emily arrives back at the welfare department complex in the late afternoon. She stays well past closing in order to plow through reams of Jackson case files detailing Joyce's long, sorry welfare history on paper. As the author I needed to break up the long chunks of case-file narrative and to account for the hours Emily spent there. I could have used the clock on the wall, but then I remembered the janitor moving through the room one evening when I had once stayed late to read case files. The character moving through the environment is not the central character, Emily, but the unnamed janitor who does his job while Emily reads. It's important to account for how vast the office was, and that she comes in at five because the chapter ends well after dark.

Emily did not pull the county car into the county lot till 4:55—well past the 4:30 deadline. She hotfooted it into the Department of Social Welfare. Family Assistance was one vast wing of this building. All the social workers and supervisors worked in a huge, fluorescent-lit, high-ceilinged room with windows along the back wall only. Their desks were set in neat groups of five with the supervisor's desk set singly nearby, like the nest of a broody mother duck. That's what Emily always thought. . . . After five pm the place cleared out, save for one other social worker who was on the phone across the acres of desks talking with a client *in extremis*. His voice rang out declamatorily in the emptiness and finally he hung up and fled. Emily was alone with the janitor, who began at the other end of the room, swinging metal trash cans into the big basket on his trash cart, where a transistor radio wailed out tinny country-western tunes into the void. Alone with the janitor and the Jackson case file. . . .

The janitor, still overturning trash cans in a fairly rhythmic manner, was close enough to her to grin when she looked up. She gave him a tiny wave, wincing when he smiled back: his mouth was a checkered array of yellow teeth and black spaces, reminding Emily of a whorehouse piano, not that she had ever played a whorehouse piano, or even seen one. . . .

The trash can clattered behind her and spun crazily on the floor, the janitor so close his radio crooned "Your Cheatin' Heart" right in her ear. Emily had not heard the janitor's approach. So deep in her reading she had heard nothing at all. And now she looked up to see the janitor victoriously emergent from Large Marge's trash can, his teeth parted over a half-eaten Hershey bar. He stepped so close to her she could all but smell the chocolate on his breath. She sat there, speechless, helpless—the man and moment frozen before her— until he moved on, pulled his cart and "Cheatin' Heart" toward the next set of desks, and Emily turned back to the files spread before her to find that what she had read and constructed into so shapely a story with some grace and grandeur was really nothing but paper lumps of sorrow and loss, infidelity and despair, defeat reeking of the jail, the latrine, the unmade bed where sweat and wet and seed and anguish all stained and stank. All this gleamed before Emily like oyster turds in the fluorescent light that hurt her eyes since full dark had fallen outside. The light itself became like water. Emily knew she was in over her head.

## Scenic Depiction to Move Characters through the Landscape

Using that same venue, the welfare department, here is a scene where Emily herself moves through the bureaucratic landscape, albeit in something of a fantasy fashion. Emily's fiancé, Rick, is far away at Georgetown Law School. The night before on their weekly Wednesday phone conversation (the story takes place in 1982), Rick has disappointed her, and they have quarreled. The following day, the receptionist at the front desk asks Emily to come out there, though she doesn't say why. This scene conjures all the emotions Emily feels as she returns to her desk.

BURNING LOVE

The ladies manning the reception desk grinned and pointed in a conspiratorial fashion to a florist's massive colorful bouquet, freesias and carnations, ferns and daisies set among the roses in glorious abundance billowing out of a blue vase. The ladies laughed and gushed that they hadn't told her because they thought it would be such a happy surprise!

"Thank you." Emily opened the diminutive card that read only "*Love, Rick.*"

She put the card back in the envelope and tried to smile. Indeed, she had no choice: she must smile. She must be joyed-over to receive flowers. Women always are. For a man to send you flowers means he loves you, a public avowal of Burning Love. Delivered here at the office, it was a public performance. Convention dictated that Emily must play her public part: blush and flush and walk back through the doors and collect the attention, the knowing smiles of all her co-workers. The young secretaries would think Emily's fiancé was just so sweet and thoughtful; the older women would know the bastard was apologizing for something. In carrying this bouquet across the vast welfare department office, Emily was publicly forgiving Rick. This evening she would have to call and thank him and he would (metaphorically) nibble on her ear through the phone. That was the way it would happen; it had all been staged. She bent her head to sniff the bouquet's heady aromas and came up light-headed, slightly nauseated, to see shimmering before her a sort of holographic Rick dressed in a white spangled bodysuit, a parody of Elvis, of Elvis's expression of passion and anguish and Elvis's posture, at once humble and dramatic.

She opened the door to the vast sea of metal desks and office workers, and before her eyes the holographic Rick jumped, spun forward and danced down the central aisle of the huge echoing emporium of ringing phones, clacking typewriters, and paper-pushing bureaucrats who were transformed. The entire office, social workers and secretaries alike all seemed to jump up on top of their gray desks, providing Rick with a triumphant choir, doo-waa-doo, ooh-waa-ooh, a perfectly pitched, soprano-wailing, bass-bounding, harmonizing gospel group. They danced and sang as Rick made his way down through the desks, as "Burning Love" ascended into the high-vaulted room and rained back down on all of them. Emily, carrying the fragrant floral chalice of his love in her arms, must follow holographic Rick's cute little bottom as it twitched away in his spangled white-sequined suit, while a chorus line of welfare workers wailed shoo-shoo-shoo-bee-doo-wah-wah. Rick sang, thump-bump-and-grinding, and Emily must rock and roll too, following her lover among the desks and admiring social workers, kicking high, showing off her flowers, visibly demonstrating to all her coworkers, to all the world the pleasure, the vindication, the validation this bouquet gave her: the triumph, excitement, expectation, desire, anticipation, jubilation, liberation, all those emotions that only Burning Love could bestow on you. When they reached Emily's desk, holographic Rick got down, got dirty, got gritty, groaned, panted, hummed hard, sang, his voice at once sweet and searing. He was going to ignite, scorch, flame up and die right here in front of her. He couldn't stop himself. Burning love. That's what it does to you.

"Nice flowers, Emily," said her supervisor, Marge.

Emily tried to say, I think they need water, but the words would not eke past the tight, closed-lipped smile she had perfected in her brace-ridden adolescence. She excused herself wordlessly and went to the women's bathroom, where she energetically crammed the flowers down the steel maw of the trash can. She tore Rick's card in shreds and dropped it in the toilet, and, since she was there, she peed.

## The Lost Domain

Let's look at a portion of a memoir by Sarah Jane Perkins recounting her childhood and youth in Depression-era Washington State. Her father had lost a leg in a logging accident in about 1927 or 1928 and now moved about with a wooden leg. To provide for his family, he bought a ramshackle, rundown hotel on the Skagit River and from here he sold bootleg hooch he made from potatoes. (This is during Prohibition.)

It might have been the Depression for everyone else, but it was fine high times for us at Watson's Landing on the Skagit River. Pa painted a sign, said Perkins Hotel, but it was always Watson's Landing. It was never ours. Pa had a neat little distillery on an island just downriver where he had a cabin set up there, high in the woods, far from the internal revenue men. He made vile hooch that sold well, especially with the steamer that stopped off twice a week at Watson's Landing. The steamer was a small shallow-bottomed flat deck boat, mainly used to fetch men and supplies back and forth from logging camps and farms upriver down to Mt. Vernon and other river towns on the flats and finally on out to Puget Sound. It tied up there just long enough for the men to have a quick stop at the hotel to buy a bottle.

The Perkinses' prosperity was swept away, and the family left destitute after a destructive flood in November 1931 ravaged western Washington. After that flood, Watson's Landing was truly a lost domain. In her memoir Sarah Jane Perkins could have described this event (more or less) as I have just above: "a destructive flood in November 1931 ravaged western Washington." But she doesn't. In the selection below she weaves her actions (the narrator's actions) together with detailed scenic depiction of the flood. Though we know that Sarah Jane survived this peril (it's a memoir, after all), her strong verbs, her vivid evocation of action, even her nonstandard presentation of dialogue combine to create a terrifying scene.

## THE RIVER AND THE RAIN

That November, Mr. Jasper got off the steamer, told them to wait at the landing while he ran up to the hotel. He told my father that steamer would not be coming back till the rain ended. The river was too high and hazardous. Mr. Jasper said to my father, I'm telling you, Amos, this is no ordinary rain. Upstream, the Skagit River is raging and gouging out new channels and with all soil and weight in it, likely when it gets down here, if the rain keeps up, it'll change course, plow itself out a whole new bank and there'll be hell to pay. It could happen anywhere along the river. It could happen here.

Mr. Jasper said we should take such cash as we had and come with him to safety downriver. At least Pa should send the Missus and us four sprouts.

Ma snorted at this. She said wasn't going to let a little rain chase her off her property, and leave every last thing she owned. . . . Pa said he would stay here, protect our property and care for the animals and we should go with Mr. Jasper. Ma said no. Said, if Pa cared to abandon his wife, then fine, he should take the children and go with Mr. Jasper. She could always make things sound like that, vile and fine, fine and vile. In the same moment.

Pa never did believe in disaster, whereas Ma believed in nothing but. But thanks to Mr. Jasper's warning, even though the steamer left without us, Pa got the boat ready, oars, buckets, stout lines and cleats, canvas for shelter. And while he was doing all that, he saw trees floating by and then he saw some cows, bloated up, bobbing down the river in the rain, half a barn and that's when he knew that Mr. Jasper was right, and upstream the river had changed its course, had carved itself out a whole new channel and that it was coming after us, and we had best get to higher ground.

Everyone to the boat, said my father. Now. We're going to the island.

It's getting dark, Amos, said my mother.

It's darker in the grave. Now, everyone to the boat. Take nothing, Sarah Jane, Pa called out to me, Just get in the boat!

I grabbed *Heidi* and *Robinson Crusoe*, presents for my tenth birthday just past. Georgieanna got the dog and her doll. Ma took such cash as we had on hand, and the baby, though he wasn't really a baby by then, but four years old and we just always called him the baby. She always carried him under one arm just like a little piglet. We all hotfooted to the boat tied up there at the landing. My brother Virgil was already there with Pa. . . .

The poplars along our bank still stood, but the river had uprooted trees upstream and you could see them churning in the roiling brown water, crashing into one another. As we clambered into the boat we could see the river had jumped banks here at Watson's Landing too, washing over our garden, and the sheds, and it was coming after the animals in the barnyard. The cow was too stupid to protest, but the hogs were outraged. The chickens squawked and flapped. Anything that couldn't climb a tree was eaten by the river, devoured by the rain. The roar was tremendous. The minute we untied from the landing, and no matter how hard Pa and Virgil rowed, we knew the river was going to take us where it would take us. And just to prove it, the river took the dog.

Never mind the dog! Make for the island! cried Pa. Virgil! Make for the island!

Pa and Virgil, kept fighting off what the river had chewed up, trees, sheds, carcasses, even an old Model T and we saw a corpse too. A woman. Her dress ballooned up, her breasts keeping her afloat like buoys. Face gray-green and awful. We didn't know her. She was gone and we let her go. We weren't too far downriver when our own sign, Perkins Hotel, floated past us. Pa kept shouting out, Make for the island! Don't let it pass, Virgil, he cried out, Make for the island!

That river was like wrestling a huge brown snake, like something biblical rising up against Sodom and Gomorrah that would eat us alive. The November afternoon was short and if we lost the light, we couldn't see the trees and debris that was coming at us and the boat would bust up and we'd drown. The island wasn't but a mile downstream and it had high ground and lots of trees and Pa knew it well.

The island came in sight, but the river didn't want to go there. Ma put the baby in Georgieanna's arms and told her to hold him and not let him go or he'd end up like the dog. She took an oar. Virgil, Pa, Ma, they fought toward that island shore, knowing if we didn't get there, it was death for us on the river. I bailed water out of the boat while they paddled and pulled and struggled and the island seemed to be going past us. Certainly the riverbank where Pa had built high pilings to tie up the boat, those were gone, drowned under. The river pulled us past all that, and still we were mid-channel and not yet close to land. I bailed and prayed, prayed and bailed and looked up at the island with every bucket I flung out of the boat. The tall trees at its summit were lost in clouds that hunkered and hovered over us, the rain still pounding. If we got swept past the island, we'd never get back to it, the current was too strong. Night was coming on. The river churned and we would be smashed up by trees and barns and boards and things we couldn't see that the river had already torn up.

Keep at it! Pa shouted. The island! Anywhere on the island!

But the island seemed to be moving past us, not us past it, as we rowed and got nowhere. Oh God, God, I prayed and bailed and by the grace of God and the power of prayer, I'm convinced, we grappled our way out of the central channel and struggled toward the rocks, the trees, the island, got close, the boat banging and shoving against unseen rocks and trees because the riverbank was gone altogether, swallowed up by the raging river, all brown and so high, that we ran right into the trees themselves.

Virgil grabbed the tow rope and leapt out, pulling with all his might, that boat against the river, pulling us up, high as he could where his feet were planted against the tree itself and he wrapped the line around the great belly of a cedar. Pa next, leaping out of the boat as best a one legged man could, holding the line with Virgil, his wooden leg sinking into the wet earth around the tree, his other foot pressed against its trunk. . . . Quick, Ma! Quick! Ma, with the baby under her arm, scrambled out. Now, you, Georgieanna! But she was crying. All right, you, Sarah Jane! Jump! Now, Georgieanna, you! Jump! Georgieanna wailing that she couldn't jump, and Pa yelling at her, Do it girl, don't look, just do it!

I went back and jumped in the boat and slapped Georgieanna a good one, pulled her out of the damned boat right behind me, and that's when I knew I was more like my mother than my father.

———

The memoir is not the story of what you know; it's the story of how you learned it. Take your reader through that learning process with the scenic vivacity your experience deserves.

# 4 | Developing Character

*All the world's a stage, and all the men and women merely players;*
*They have their exits and their entrances;*
*And one man in his time plays many parts.*
—Shakespeare, As You Like It, 1599

Not coincidentally, the word *character* refers to made-up people in a play or a novel and a set of human qualities. We speak of a person's character as opposed to personality. We speak of a person as having good character; we don't say they have good personality. They might have *a* good personality, singular, suggesting a pleasing social presence, but that doesn't touch the churning cauldron of values, choices, decisions, delusions and loyalties, loves and ambivalence that, over time, create bedrock character. Character is complex, and cannot be wholly ascribed to, nor derived from, nor reflected in one's economic circumstances, familial, religious, ethnic, geographical, or professional identity. Though the people in the pages of your memoir are real people who walked the earth, on the page they become characters, like in a novel, or a play: the reader develops feelings for and about them. As characters they need to be developed. The people in your memoir may romp through your memory, but the responsibility lies with you, the author, to make them vivid on the page.

Beginning with what they look like. Sometimes the people you know the best are the ones who elude description. When I went back east to grad school someone there asked me what my mother looked like. I was astonished at my inability to describe her, a person I knew so well. Though I could see her face before me, I could say little beyond that, like me, she had dark hair and dark eyes. (Conversely, had I been asked what my sixth grade teacher looked like, I could have done that in a flash! Think on it: the faces you know the best are the ones you cannot describe. Those who touch your life briefly make a visual impact.) Netta Gibbs's failure to describe Granny and Joe in that swift, early segment of her memoir is understandable, given the above, but the lack of description diminishes their vivacity. Sarah Jane Perkins does right by the flood, but she didn't really *describe* anyone in that boat, certainly not Georgieanna or Virgil; Pa's wooden leg, Ma's broad shoulders, yes we could see these. (To be fair, Sarah Jane had described Pa and Ma in earlier chapters; that river sequence was excerpted from a larger memoir.)

Aside from hair, eyes, body type, age, any scars, impediments, and the like, physical description emanates from the ways in which people carry their bodies. The ways in which they go through the world, the way their passions or professions inform their physical presence: the accountant, the musician, the homeless person, the Bob Cratchits of the world as opposed to the Ebenezer Scrooges. (Indeed, Dickens is one of the great describers of literature.) Do they walk with the easy lope of the athlete or the gingery tread of the uncertain? For some people, a slouch indicates a mental attitude as well. For some, a broad, swaying stride indicates a relationship to the rest of the world, perhaps even only a wished-for relationship to the rest of the world. Timid people practically percolate their insecurities. Anyone who has ever taught a class, or waited tables, or worked in retail knows that, physically, certain people give off a sunny vibe or its opposite. Personality, even a bit of character, can sometimes be suggested by the kinds of clothes people wear and the way they wear them: the dapper businessman, the fashion plate, the woman who always seems to look like a museum guard no matter what she's wearing. Mr. Flannel can be pretty much interchangeable with Ms. Flannel. (I only met Mr. and Ms. Flannel when I moved to the Pacific Northwest; they didn't live in Southern California. However, Mr. Beach Dude and Ms. Tie Dye lived there, and when I was in college, a clean T-shirt and clean jeans were considered the height of both fashion and hygiene.)

What about deeper character, in the sense of "good character?" How is it possible to portray that on the page? Indelible characters are the result of the writer's ability to provide specific details so that people's dialogue, their actions and choices, deepen what we know of them. It's not enough for the narrator to say: "xxxx was a monster." The reader needs to see that person engaged in cruel acts, and making cruel choices. British/Canadian writer Helen Forrester wrote three volumes of memoirs describing her wretched youth in Depression-era Liverpool, England. Unlike Frank McCourt's family who had never known anything but poverty, Helen Forrester's family had been well-to-do, flung into homeless misfortune through her parents' squanderous bad choices. Helen, the eldest, was twelve at the time. In that first memoir, *Twopence to Cross the Mersey*, the narrator never says her mother was a monster, but the mother's actions convinced this reader that the mother was trying to kill Helen, that there were too many children to feed, that Helen was expendable, that starvation and neglect would suffice to get rid of her. The actions of Frank McCourt's parents, by contrast, seem feckless, drunken, selfish, and irresponsible, but not intentionally monstrous.

Though we can all at one time or another be feckless, drunken, selfish, and irresponsible, character plays out over time, and indeed, character can alter over time as, say, the youthful rebel emerging into middle age (a homeowner, a family man) as a conservative clinging to the very values he had spurned as a kid. Think of a character like Michael Corleone in *The Godfather*, early on telling his girlfriend that he's not like the rest of the family. Subsequent events and choices propel him from that statement into the very pinnacle (or the very depths) of his family.

Like individuals, long-term relationships, whether of family, friend-ship, lovers, and even coworkers, are complex. Nothing in any rela-tionship stays completely the same without wrinkle or blemish even when respect and affection endure. Relationships go through varie-gated moments, some affected by small-time spats (control of the TV remote, the trash not taken out) to family phalanxes lined up against each other, serious quarrels over money, inheritance, divorce, in-laws, drugs, or alcohol. Relationships outside of family alter and attenuate when circumstances change; experiences like combat or natural disasters, or even parenting kids as they go through their school years, often create intense relationships that later fray or weaken, leaving perhaps a sense of loyalty, even affection, but not connection.

## Prompt: Late of this Parish

To convey complicated people and complex relationships in a memoir, the author sometimes needs to step back from the story itself. To look at the characters in a way intrinsically aimed at finding understanding. "Late of This Parish" takes its title from Charles Dickens's *Great Expectations*, that brilliant opener when Pip goes to the graveyard and meets the fearsome convict Magwitch. Magwitch demands to know where his parents are, and Pip points to the tombstones behind him and says, "Here, sir, late of this parish." We will, so to speak, make your characters "late of this parish": first dispatch them, and then develop them. The people you are writing about certainly do not need to have left this life for this prompt to help you as a writer.

Choose a character, a person from your piece in progress. Then approach that individual in four separate steps. Write:

1. AN OBITUARY of the sort that might appear in a newspaper, briefly noting the basic elements, even the legalisms of their life: when they are born, to whom, where, where educated, service, job, marriage(s), children, grandchildren, and so on.
2. A EULOGY. Eulogies are generally very forgiving. The individual eulogized—that is, the Dearly Departed—is always described in the best possible light. Eulogies make only glancing reference to their shortcomings; that person's occasionally feckless, drunken, selfish, irresponsible episodes are largely veiled, and the good qualities highlighted and remembered. The eulogy presents the shining best. If you remember in *Tom Sawyer*, the town thinking Huck and Tom have died, hold a memorial service for them and the boys, hovering close enough to overhear, get misty just hearing

how wonderful they were and how everyone loved them . . . now that they're gone. Write for your character a eulogy.

3. AN ANTI-EULOGY. Here we also take our cue from Mark Twain, who, when he wanted to marry the well-to-do Olivia Langdon, was obliged by her father to submit character references. Twain asked the three people who detested him most (including the novelist Bret Harte) to write on his behalf. These letters surprised Mr. Langdon considerably. But Twain pointed out that, having read these, Mr. Langdon would know the worst of him. Write for your character an anti-eulogy.

4. LASTLY, CHOOSE A SCENE FROM THIS LIFE AND WRITE IT UP. In creating the scene, be certain that *elements of your obit, your eulogy, and your anti-eulogy are all three vivid and present.* That is, some notion of the character's historical moment and context. Some element of the positive elements in their character. Some element of the not-so-positive, the downright negative. Use this scene to expand and deepen your understanding, your portrayal of your characters and their true, bedrock character. Writing a eulogy and an anti-eulogy can offer the writer of memoir context that emotion, retrospect, or caution might obscure. Writers of fiction too can use "Late of This Parish" to deepen and create characters.

While no single scene can encapsulate a whole life or the entire person, one of the most memorable presentations of "Late of This Parish" was written by a student in one of my University of Washington classes. Her (still living) father was a storekeeper who, in the course of some thirty-plus years, went on to hold important civic positions in their township, including being on the board of education. She imagined the eulogy given by the mayor, or the superintendent of instruction, or some such civic worthy who extolled her father as a pillar of the community, reciting his many contributions to the municipal good. (Indeed, her father sounded like the very sort of Good Citizen Ben Franklin's *Autobiography* portrayed.) For the anti-eulogy, the writer imagined herself in the church pew, listening to the praise lavished on her father, and thinking how her father had cultivated the assumption of his own importance at the expense of his family, how he demanded that the family should circle endlessly in his glowing orbit, how the moral support, kindness, time, and effort he gave to the town, he took, in a manner of speaking, from his wife and children.

The *scene* she created from the eulogy and the anti-eulogy was simple, a family dinner on an ordinary weeknight; the simplicity was part of its power: she titled it something uncomplicated, like "Suppertime." The scene itself never left the kitchen, so the scenic depiction was spare and easily accomplished. The father always insisted that the family must eat at 5:30 so the father could attend his civic meetings, but this evening dinner is late due to unforeseen circumstances. The kitchen is full of tension as the mother hurries to get supper on the table and the narrator and her brother set the table. Once they finally sit down to eat, the father berates the narrator's brother, who has been caught up in some minor scrape at school. The rest of the scene is largely related in dialogue as Dad castigates the boy not simply for his bad behavior, but because his misbehavior reflects on the father, something along the lines of "What will people think of me if my son gets in trouble? I can't have you humiliating me." In this scene no one raised their voice. No one fought back. No one challenged the father. Dinner finished, the father took his coat and the family car, and he left to lead the school-board meeting. The reader understood all.

———

I am always astonished to read, as with "Suppertime," how often the eulogy and the anti-eulogy reflect the same set of traits told from different perspectives. Take the story of the Ant and the Grasshopper. Traditionally, it goes something like this:

An Ant was spending a frosty winter's day drying grain he had collected during the summertime. A Grasshopper, dying of hunger, passed by and earnestly begged for a little food. The Ant inquired of him, "Why did you not stock up on food during summer?"

The Grasshopper replied, "I had no time. I passed my days singing."

The Ant then said in derision, "If you are foolish enough to sing all summer, you'll dance supperless to bed in winter."

This traditional fable favors the Ant. That the Ant has acted correctly is the point of the story; indeed, the moral of the story. The Ant is smug, but justified. The Grasshopper is pathetic, and properly turned away. The eulogy and the anti-eulogy might reveal nuances the fable doesn't address.

Briefly, the eulogy for the Ant might read:

Casper P. Ant was an ant of great prudence and integrity. He was always diligent, loyal, and painstaking. His bosses admired him, and he more than once was Employee of the Month. He asked no special favors and he gave none, but he could be always relied upon to do the correct thing. Casper was an ant of few words and kept his own wise counsel.

The Ant's anti-eulogy might read:

Casper P. Ant kept his antennae to the grindstone no matter what. He clocked in, and when he clocked out—of life itself— few will miss him. He took no special joy, not even in a job well done. He distrusted levity of any sort. His wife and children were a sad, wizened lot. He seldom joined friends informally, though he attended company picnics and winter socials where he could hardly eke out a smile while others laughed at jokes, or applauded the music. He had a pinched heart, and he kept accounts of every bit of grass and grain that came into or went out of his house. He prided himself on his own probity. An ant of little sympathy.

What would be the best scene to illuminate these qualities? A day on the job? A winter social where he can be seen to be distrusting of any levity? A ceremony where Caspar is awarded Employee of the Month and his wife and children smile meekly, anxious that someone might crack a joke and Caspar be offended?

And for the Grasshopper? His eulogy might read:

> James (Jimbo) G. Grasshopper lit up any place he chanced to be. He had charisma and talent. At any gathering where the beer flowed, he was known to drink with the best of them, and as he played his famous fiddle, toes would tap and hands would clap, and spirits lighten. Jimbo knew more jokes than anyone, and he could make just about anyone smile. His charm made the girls all feel pretty, and the guys all feel worthy. He was a bright flame and many warmed themselves near his brightness.

And the anti-eulogy:

> James P. Grasshopper was a bright light, but a shallow insect, interested only in himself. He was cavalier in all things, trusting to his charm, his luck, and his looks to provide whatever he needed. He seemed to think he automatically deserved any good done to or for him. He literally fiddled away his many gifts. His need to collect applause, to be the center of attention, was all but insatiable. He claimed to have a vast array of friends, but in truth, he always settled for simple admirers. He had many girlfriends, but never married, and there is no known next of kin.

What would be the best scene to illuminate these qualities? Some gathering where Jimbo hogged the spotlight while he raised the spirits of everyone around him? Or where, perhaps someone needed from him something more than a tune and a whistle, perhaps that person needed genuine caring that he could not give? Some instance perhaps where he forsook a lover in his search for new admiring audiences?

Another possibility for a scene with both the Ant and the Grasshopper might well be where Jimbo is performing at a big Ant Picnic in the summertime, and the music and his fiddling and dancing rev up the usually hardworking ants, a gathering where Jimbo's gifts have value, have merit, and are much appreciated. If that's so, if the ants once enjoyed what he had to offer, if they reveled in his gifts, then Casper's refusal in Jimbo's moment of need, his smugness reflects badly on him, even granting that Jimbo has been cavalier, irresponsible, and possibly drunken.

———

Let us look at a life far more complex than that of the Grasshopper or the Ant, one where the individual lived in many places, undertook many different ventures, and touched many lives in one way or another.

OBIT: Mason Douglass, 1898–1970, born in frontier Idaho, the youngest son of six children in a Mormon family. His father died when Mason was a toddler. His mother brought the family to St. Elmo, California, in 1900 where he graduated from high school in 1916. When America entered World War I, Mason joined the US Army and served honorably in France. In 1920 he became an aide to Congressman Eustace P. Giddings. While in Washington, DC, he married Margaret Denton, who survives him along with their two children and four grandchildren.

EULOGY: Mason Douglass was meticulous, industrious, and congenial. Though his high-pitched voice precluded a career in politics, still, he served his country, fighting in France in World War I and working in Washington for Congressman Eustace P. Giddings. Here he made a name for himself as a ready listener, a man to get things done. He could turn observation into inspiration. He was a shrewd investor, always alert to the potential for growth and expansion particularly in property, livestock, and mineral rights. Later in life his acumen took him to various outposts of enterprise including Colorado, Florida, Idaho, and Alberta, Canada. He founded many companies and made himself and others rich. And when he lost money, he did so with grace, and always unbowed, sought out the next adventure.

ANTI-EULOGY: Mason Douglass was a freelance larcenist. He started out working for Congressman Giddings, graduated to being a lobbyist, and went on from there to become a fraud and a huckster. He had a genius for the use of other people's money. He knew how to curry favor and peddle influence. He manipulated bonds, promissory notes, pledges, deeds, trusts, and investments, and he recognized that the rustle of this kind of paper and a few big words could play on the guileless aspirations of any old yahoo, fill them with remunerative visions beyond their wildest dreams. The unsuspecting ranch hand, the educated banker, Mason Douglass cheated them all, regardless of race, creed, or color. When his schemes collapsed, he moved fast, often just ahead of the law, leaving ruin behind him.

SCENE:


## REVELATIONS

Mason joined his friend Revelation Pinckney after dinner one evening strolling downtown St. Elmo to attend a political rally for the Sixth Congressional district candidate. Revelation was born plain Harold Pinckney, but he was called Revelation because he had a passion for politics. Mason cared nothing for politics, but he went along because it was a Saturday night and he had nothing else to do.

"Un-canny, that's what they say about me," Revelation confided, "but I tell 'em, it ain't like a gift of God or nuthin. All it takes in politics is a little expurience, a lot of smarts, and some footwork." He regarded his foot as if he expected it to testify on his behalf. "I'm telling you, Mason, the future for a really smart guy, in this day and age, 1920, right now! Is in politics! Republican politics. Do you follow me?"

"Sure, sure," said Mason, knowing that with his squeaky, high-pitched voice he had no future in politics.

"The Demmycrats, they ain't nothing but a bunch of lily-livered Gentiles ready to hand the country over to the settlement workers and the Pope. But the Republicans, they are the hundred-percenters, the real Amur'cans!" Revelation said as they came to the back of a large crowd before a bunting-clad platform where the candidate, Eustace P. Giddings, flanked on either side by notables, rose and stepped to the podium.

Giddings was the choice of the Republicans to replace the eighty-two-year-old senile incumbent. Giddings was distinguished and attractive, his blond hair having faded to a tinsely gray and his deep-set eyes suggestive of great thoughts. He stared at the podium momentarily as if his speech were written in the original Hebrew and he'd have to translate. His voice was golden. "My friends, there are those in Washington who still don't believe in the election of a Latter-day Saint to Congress, who say that the Saints don't keep faith with the Constitution, don't keep the Church and State separate. I say unto you, these people are fools! Everyone knows the Good Saint and the Good Citizen are one and the same! We need a righteous man in Washington to represent the will of righteous men!" Wild applause greeted him.

Having no gift for public speaking, Mason endured twenty solid minutes in the grip of green envy while Giddings collected bouts of applause. Then his attention drifted to the sleek, mute, prosperous Republicans sitting on the platform behind the candidate, men of influence, stature, gold watch chains looped across their well-fed bellies. Something flickered for Mason, not revelation exactly, but inspiration. Studying the gentlemen sitting there he wondered if perhaps Revelation was right, and he, Mason, had thought of politics too narrowly. Why shouldn't he be up there with those men? Mason had seen Paree; he had tasted wine and women. Why should he be living his with mother? Why should he be clerking in a dry-goods store, sweeping up, stocking shelves, chafing in a job utterly unworthy of him? He had an ambitious vision of himself, field boots caked with alkali, binoculars in hand, armed with charts and maps framed by desolate mountains, and surrounded by raw, shiny mining machinery. On the strength of that vision, he had applied to the Colorado School of Mines and just that week had been rejected.

The next morning, clad in a dark suit he borrowed from his older brother, Mason presented himself, squeaky voice and all, at Giddings's hotel suite. He introduced himself as Mason Douglass: Republican, Latter-day Saint, veteran of the Great War, awarded the Purple Heart, and a graduate of the Colorado School of Mines. He smiled, shook hands all round, and offered his services to the campaign and beyond, a man who would dedicate himself to Eustace Giddings and an era of ongoing Republican ascendancy.

This scene describing an incident in Mason's young manhood tells us something from his obit (it situates him in St. Elmo, California, where he grew up, and that he fought in the Great War). In this scene we see a pivotal shift that reflects both the eulogy and the anti-eulogy. In the words of the eulogy, we see here a man "alert to the potential for growth," who "turned observation into inspiration." Also, a la the eulogy, having identified this possible path to advancement, Mason acts on it immediately, showing up the very next morning at Giddings's hotel, smiling, affable, full of go-to zeal, knowing instinctively "how to curry favor." We also see evidence of the anti-eulogy in his unblinking lie about the Purple Heart, and being a graduate of the Colorado School of Mines which had rejected him outright. Only a small leap of the imagination is required to envision the man who moved fast when his schemes collapsed, often just ahead of the law, leaving ruin behind him.

---

Developing characters means developing scenes in which these people can act, in which their choices and their dialogue express the jumbled impulses that swirl inside each of us. We are all less like the sparkling blue, chlorinated swimming pool, and more like the sea, a tumble of amber sand and rusty kelp, broken shells, pale driftwood, floating debris, darting fish, and random chance awash in a saline green, at the mercy of, whether we like it or not, the tides of time. All of us wash up on the shores of memory.

# 5 | Did He Really Say That?

*In this book a number of dialects are used. . . . The shadings have
not been done in a haphazard fashion, or by guesswork; but painstakingly
and with the trustworthy guidance and support of personal familiarity
with these several forms of speech. I make this explanation for the reason
that without it many readers would suppose that all these characters
were trying to talk alike and not succeeding.*
—Mark Twain's Explanatory Note to *The Adventures of Huckleberry Finn*, 1885

D id he really say that? Are these the words that actually tumbled
from her lips? Can you possibly remember precisely what people said in the past? The answer to these questions is a resounding
*no*. However, the memoir is not the courtroom where the testimony
is sworn to. The memoir is the creation of a writer who evokes the
elusive past and animates the people in it. People carry their pasts
around in their voices, their word choice, their diction, their accents.
The point of giving them dialogue is not to recall verbatim every word
spoken, but to evoke the tone, the richness and ripple of these voices,
what they said, and how they spoke. The characters in your memoir
do not need to sound like Winston Churchill or Maya Angelou to
have their own kind of eloquent, indelible voices. Dialogue is artificial. Voice is authentic.

In any work of prose—fiction or nonfiction—the function of dialogue is three-fold: (1) to reveal character; (2) to develop tension; and
(3) to convey mood, meaning, and information that will further or
deepen the story.

Every exchange of dialogue in your pages ought to fulfill at least
one of these functions.

Creating strong dialogue relies on four major foundations:

*1. Spoken conversation is not—repeat not—the equivalent of written dialogue.* Spoken conversation is often rambling, repetitive, and boring. Dialogue cannot be. On the page, even the most cursory, casual exchange is important. Dialogue is an artificial narrative construct to help shape and enrich your story.

For the best example of just how rambling, repetitive, and boring conversation can be, you have only to glance through the transcripts of the Watergate tapes published in book form. The reader knows historically that a profound constitutional crisis is unfolding on the page, but these men and their conversation are banal and boring; they blather, swear, go off on tangents, come back, touch upon, go off again . . .

In ordinary conversation, people interrupt, overlap, chime in, and bow out all the time. Conversation is constantly peppered with "you know, you know, you know . . ." with "no, really?" with unnecessary "like," with inane expletives. Consider, for instance, how long it takes to get off the phone, especially, say, with a close friend. You agree to "talk soon" over and over, not so much for clarity as to hear the other person's general assent. You make fleeting references, about any number of things. ("Sure, Tuesday's fine, unless my car dies again. I don't trust it anymore." "I know what you mean! Mine, well the radiator last week . . ." "Oh god, right! Well . . .") Then of course "love you" is exchanged several times along with "take care" and finishing up perhaps with some warm family name or shorthand exchange of affection. Transcribed exactly, this would take up *whole pages* and would offer *nothing* to develop tension; to deepen and reveal character; and to convey mood, meaning, or information.

Dialogue, as opposed to spoken conversation, must be groomed and shaped to create *effect*. Dialogue is artificial; it's the writer's responsibility to make it sound organic, to make voices ring true.

2. THE WRITER IS NOT A DIRECTOR. THE WRITER IS NOT A SCREEN-WRITER. THE WRITER IS THE WRITER. I am sorry to tell you, dear writer, that you do not have a gaggle of gifted actors to express mean-

ing, emotion, intent, nuance, irony, sarcasm, or profound depth of feeling with their eyes, their facial expressions, and the harmonic gradations of their resonant voices. Alas, dear writer, you have no innate visual cues. You have what is on the page, and *only* what is on the page.

So go easy on the facial and physical descriptions. Too much shrugging, frowning, blinking, chin stroking, face scrunching, blah blah blah, totally gets in the way of the dialogue. He shrugged his shoulders. She drew her brows together. He pinched his lips. She raised her eyebrows in a surprised manner. He shook his head in a worried fashion. Her eyes widened with fear. Line after line like this bores readers and detracts from what your people are *saying*, particularly if you offer up these facial descriptions after every sentence actually spoken. The reader's attention goes to imagining what the hands and shoulders and nose and eyebrows are doing and not what is actually being *said*.

Get rid of this stuff. Let your dialogue itself do the heavy lifting.

3. RELAX THE RULES OF GRAMMAR. Most people don't speak in semicolons. In writing dialogue, you can have lots of run-on sentences to be true to the voice you're portraying. You can have weird pronunciation. ("Pass 'em biskits and be quick 'bout it.") Bad grammar is fine. ("He come to church for the coffee and donuts, and no other reason.") The key to creating an authentic voice is consistency in rendering dialogue.

4. DICTION IS CHARACTER. DICTION ENHANCES CHARACTER. The people in your memoir are your own people. You can surely hear their voices. You're not transcribing their speech like a court reporter; you're catching the flavor of it, the texture, the idiosyncratic shorthand references that pepper their speech, their lapses of grammar or good manners. Speech patterns, choice of metaphors, or similes indicate character and give depth. All of this makes for lively reading, imbues them with vivacity, individuality. Whoever they are, you do not want your people to sound like bland, homogenized, standard-issue television newscasters. In creating dialogue for the people in your

memoir, remember how they expressed themselves, how their speech might have been full of regional or ethnic or cultural eccentricities.

## Codes, Clichés, Clusters of Expression

Consider Melville's famous story *Bartleby*. The title character has only one phrase, one repeated line of dialogue throughout: "I would prefer not to." But just imagine for a moment, the vast swath of coloration such a phrase has. How many ways are there to say "I would prefer not to"? Consider the diction of the church lady, of the kid from Compton, of the giddy twenty-something Influencer, of the judge, or of the waitress who has been on her feet all day. How would each of these people say "I would prefer not to"?

All families or longtime friends/relationships have their own codes often unknown or weird to others, internal phrases and clichés that form a kind of shorthand. Lovers often use names and endearments inexplicable to others. I have a friend whose affectionate banter with her husband includes the phrase, "You stink." And doesn't everyone have a friend who comes into the house exclaiming, "Greetings, you filthy animals!" Often the eldest grandchild gets to name the grandparents who, for the rest of their lives, become Gommie and Gompie, or Goomah. Nicknames, affectionate names, will resonate for lifetimes. Childish words and phrases outside the family context can be baffling, but once people are absorbed into a realm of affection, then everyone signs off with Bunnyhugs. Certain expressions become a kind of shorthand. In our family the phrase "owl shit" speaks volumes; the origin is from the phrase "xxxx is just as weird as owl shit" (though I have no idea why owl shit should be especially weird). Certain sayings carry family baggage that indicates deeper values or practices. In one family a child flapping his lips might be told to "Save your breath to cool your soup." In another, "Children are to be seen, not heard." Or simply, "Didn't I tell you to shut up?" In some families, the phrase, "I'm going to take off my slipper and beat you," is a cause for fear. In others, it's a hyperbolic indication of minor, loving vexation.

Speech filled with biblical allusion tells you not that the person is a religious nut, but that they have an internal set of cues, shorthand for themes, actions, emotions. The bible is full of expressions that have wended their way into everyday English (though I do think that is changing for new generations). Still, gradations of biblical reference can convey character and background. The person who in a moment of shock or anxiety says, "Oh great God in heaven!" or "Amen!" probably has a different frame of reference than the person who says merely, "Oh god," or the person who says, "Holy shit." Some with Catholic backgrounds might say, "Jesus, Mary, and Joseph!" When I created devout Mormon characters for my novel *These Latter Days*, they needed phrases to express anger, anxiety, but clearly they couldn't use standard blasphemy. Mirroring the Catholic "Jesus, Mary, and Joseph!" I gave them the phrase, "Jesus, Joseph, and Emma!" (As in the Latter-day Saint founder, Joseph Smith, and his first wife, Emma.) For the non-Mormon in the novel, Doctor Tipton, he too could not have used ordinary blasphemy in a Mormon town. For him I created the phrase, "Galloping Gallstones!"

When you endow your speakers with these sorts of endemic expressions, you convey background. Once introduced, you can continue to use these phrases to dramatic effect. For instance, in *Angela's Ashes*, Frank McCourt makes plain that when his father comes home late at night, rouses the boys, and makes them promise to "Die for Ireland," these speeches inform the reader that the father is drunk. The "Die for Ireland" speeches are a sort of shorthand, and far more vivid and effective than if McCourt wrote: *My dad came home drunk night after night and woke us up and made us repeat patriotic promises.*

As you endow the people in your memoir with these sorts of familial phrases or constructions, you will be inviting your reader into their frame of reference and, especially as the work grows, that frame of reference will resonate.

In writing dialogue, do not fear clichés. "That's the straw that broke the camel's back." Your English teacher might have circled it in red. Indeed, I would circle it red if it were in narration. But in dialogue?

Hey, if that's how your old grandpa speaks, then so be it. Don't let anyone tell you differently. Clichés are fine in dialogue; they convey character and circumstance.

Sometimes phrases, particularly from an immigrant past, will echo in the verbal patterns for generations. I have a childhood friend whose grandparents emigrated from Italy as young people; their English was good, though heavily inflected. Quite apart from accent, they spoke in odd constructions. "Close the light," her grandfather always said, instead of "turn off the light." "Close the light" is still the chosen phrase in her family. When my mother wrote *Centennial Memoir*, she included a section of Armenian phrases that were commonplace in our family. I was surprised that so many of the phrases/nouns/expressions I took for granted were actually Armenian in origin. They were just part of our parlance. *Keebar* means high class, first rate. *Parovyless* means congratulations. *Gerjejook* means old person, as in, to convey someone's driving, or to explain a lapse: "I am getting gerjejook." *Pernich* means potholder. My children, too, use many of these phrases with their spouses and friends. (And there has been more than one kitchen emergency when someone had to quickly learn what *pernich* meant!)

Nonnative speakers of English carry their own challenges in creating dialogue. Beware of overdoing and, equally, underdoing. Caricature of a French speaker, for example, posits the fact that the French don't have "th" sound, so they pronounce it badly, a la Pepé Le Pew, *Zees ees zee way we speak, Zees eez zee way you do zees.* Not only does this look stupid on paper, it calls undue attention to itself, which means it becomes an obstacle to understanding. When creating speech for nonnative speakers, honor their syntax.

In Ernest Hemingway's *A Farewell to Arms*, the main character, Frederick Henry, is an American living among Italian soldiers and fighting on the Italian front in World War I. When these soldiers speak, when Frederick speaks to them or with them, Hemingway observes their speech formally. For instance, in English, we say "I *am* twenty years old," or "I *am* hungry," or "I *am* thirsty"; in Italian (as in

French and other Latin languages), these sentences are constructed thus: I *have* twenty years. I *have* thirst. I *have* hunger. Hemingway wrote the Italians' dialogue in this fashion, honoring their syntax, so readers know they are reading exchanges in Italian.

Another brilliant solution to rendering heavily accented English can be found in Gerald Durrell's *My Family and Other Animals*, a lush, lovely memoir of an English family's sojourn on Corfu in the 1930s. Spiro, an islander who becomes a close family friend, has some English, but it is idiosyncratic. Durrell renders everything Spiro says in the plural; nouns, verbs, everything: "Yous" and "Theys." The unique construction continually imparts the flavor, the cadence of Spiro's speech, and yet his meanings are never unclear.

Sometimes foreign phrases seep into language, become embedded there, quite apart from their origins. My father had a favorite swear phrase, "Judas Priest All Friday H!" I had no idea what it meant, none of us did, other than that Dad was pissed off, or shocked, or somehow at his wits end. Even my dad didn't know what it meant. (I asked him.) A few years ago I was leafing through Eric Partridge's *Dictionary of Slang and Unconventional Usage* (a tome, by the way, that is absolutely Unputdownable!) when I stumbled on Judas Priest. It was a corruption of the French phrase *jeu d'esprit* that was picked up by British and American soldiers fighting in France in World War I. Two of my father's uncles fought in France in that conflict and brought home foreign phrases (and probably much else) unknown in Idaho in 1920. "All Friday H"? I still have no idea. My dad had other iconic phrases that reflected his Depression-era childhood in Idaho. "What won't fatten will fill." Or my favorite, a phrase that resonates with his staunchly Mormon background, "No rest for the wicked, and the righteous don't need it!" "Close the door! Were you born in a barn?" This phrase might have been learned from his father who was, in fact, born in a dugout in frontier Idaho.

If the people in your memoir speak with particularly countrified diction, or where their speech is an admixture of cultural influences, feel free to make your spelling conform to the sound you want achieve.

Be alert, however, to the perils of overdoing nonstandard diction. You don't want your characters to come off as stereotypes. You don't want to write in such a way that their speech is hard to read. A few phrases consistently rendered can imbue the whole character.

Sometimes in rendering dialogue that is historically correct, you might need to offer some additional clarity. My novel, *The Music Room*, set 1969–1970, is an intimate story with a small cast of characters, including a pair of hippie lovers. They would refer to one another casually as "my old lady" or "my old man," which in that era meant "my boyfriend" or "my girlfriend." The copyeditor on the book was confounded by these phrases, since they usually denote an offhand reference to one's mother or father. I debated cutting the phrases altogether, but they added authenticity to the story. So I clarified briefly when we first met these characters.

> "Tim, these are my nieces, Marcella and Rose-Renee. Girls, this is my old man, Tim."
>
> "That isn't your father," Marcella frowned. "Your father's in Florida."
>
> "What do you want me to say, squirt? He's my beau?" Linda gave a rippling laugh. "Tim and I are together."
>
> "That we are babycakes." He smiled.

## Diction Choices in Rendering Dialogue

Speech reflects educational level, but most Americans, even the best-educated, speak in an easy conversational style. "Wanna see a movie?" rather than "Would you like to see a movie with me?" "Wanna meet there at six?" rather than "Would you like to meet there at six?" Most American dialogue will be read, absorbed in a casual fashion without using *gonna*, *wanna*, and so forth. If, on the page, you actually write dialogue using *gonna*, *wanna*, *coulda*, *woulda*, these phrases have far more significance than they would in a casual spoken exchange. They matter because they reflect on the speaker. The person who on the page says "I wish I could have went with you" is telling the reader *reams* of information.

Easy conversational style might well also mean leaving the "g" off of certain words. "I have nothing to say about that," would probably come out, "I have nothin' to say about that."

"Are you coming too?" might actually sound like, "Are you comin' too?" As with *gonna, wanna, coulda,* once you start using these constructions in *dialogue,* they have more weight and meaning than in mere conversation. If you have a character who habitually speaks this way, instead of sprinkling your page with apostrophes (comin', nothin', goin'), it's more effective to just endow that speaker with the way the words actually sound and leave off the apostrophes. (After a while they start to look like pepper spilled across the page.) Better to have your character say "nuthin" (rather than nothin'), or "That was really sumthin!" Just serve up the word the way it would have been said. The reader will pick up the rhythm of this speech. With any of these constructions in rendering dialogue, you must remain consistent for this person. As long as you do, your reader will absorb them effortlessly. (However, if you publish, you might want to alert the copyeditor that your unconventional constructions are intentional and should not be messed with. I speak from experience.)

Even if your people are of the same age, the same social situations, or the same educational and ethnic and regional background, their personalities will be reflected in different speech patterns. The bossy little girl speaks differently from her shy, insecure classmate. The diffident, the intrinsically self-effacing express these characteristics vocally. In the below exchange (c. 1924) a young family man, Gideon Douglass, is saying good-bye to his uncle, Fred Douglass, whom Gideon has not seen since he was just a child. Fred, a drifter now, found Gideon, but he will only stay for dinner, not more. The reader can sense from Fred's dialogue his unease and evasion, but also his roundabout way of conveying some element of the truth in answer to his nephew's parting question.

"I don't mean to make you go through it all over again, Fred, but I have to know," Gideon implored him. "How did Father die? How did it happen?"

They stood in a pool of light under a streetlamp, and Fred watched the moths. "Well, Gideon, who can say? Things like that just happen to some folks, and they don't happen to others. It's real hard to figure out, if you're not too smart, like me. It was Samuel was the smart one." Fred coughed and spat. "But I'll tell you the truth, Gideon, it was an awful thing that happened to your father."

"Did he suffer much?"

"Well, yes, I think he did. We all do, but there's some suffer more than others, and there's those who don't even know they're suffering till the suffering comes to be all they know, and Samuel was one of those. I mean, I think he was." Fred took a deep breath and another licorice bit. "And that house. Well, it's gone, I guess. Long gone, and I don't exactly know how it happened to be burnt, as you say, but anything can burn, you know, given the heat and the flame, and no one could rescue Samuel, Gideon. No one could get to him before he burned up in a fire maybe even of his own making."

"His own making?"

"His own carelessness or thoughtlessness, Gideon. Samuel was often careless and thoughtless. I got to go now. The train. Timetables don't lie. You know that." He reached for Gideon's hand but threw his arms around him instead. "I always knew you'd make something of yourself, and you turned out just like I woulda wished. I couldn't ask for more." He patted Gideon resolutely, turned and ambled toward the station.

In creating conversation out of dialogue, the writer might do well to remember that women are generally more inclusive than men. Men, especially if they outnumber the women, often habitually interrupt women. Some people are instinctively conciliatory, some are instinctively competitive, and some enjoy creating shock waves.

I've always thought that F. Scott Fitzgerald's use of conversation in the opening pages of *The Great Gatsby* brilliantly illuminates these characters' personalities as well as their bedrock character. None of this dialogue is earth-shaking, or confessional or deep, but all of it is revelatory. In that opener, Nick (the first-person narrator) goes to the Buchanan's palatial home late one afternoon in June, introducing the reader to Tom, Daisy, and Jordan, three main characters. Daisy is Nick's second cousin, and he had known her husband, Tom Buchanan, at Yale. Jordan Baker, a young, athletic pro golfer, is a friend of Daisy's. The scene is long and leisurely, astutely rendered, weaving visuals, metaphors, ambience, and observations, such as Tom Buchanan's body being "capable of enormous leverage—a cruel body." Even to disregard the supporting narration, and look only at the dialogue itself, reveals depths, and perhaps more importantly, shallows. (By the way, I can actually quote this dialogue because in 2021 *The Great Gatsby* entered the public domain!)

As they go into dinner, and someone is about to light the candles, Daisy remarks wistfully, "'Do you always watch for the longest day of the year and then miss it? I always watch for the longest day of the year and then miss it.'"

Jordan offers, "'We ought to plan something.'"

"'All right,' said Daisy. 'What'll we plan?' She turned to me helplessly. 'What do people plan?'"

The cruelty implied in the description of Tom's body is borne out by his dialogue at dinner where he regales his guests with dire assertions he has gleaned from some book he read called *The Rise of the Colored Empires*. Amid her husband's oration, Daisy leans over and whispers to Nick, "'I'll tell you a family secret . . . It's about the butler's nose. Do you want to hear about the butler's nose?'"

Nick gallantly replies, "'That's why I came over tonight.'"

This light exchange effectively punctures Tom's pompous pronouncements on *The Rise of the Colored Empires*, though more bluster and banter ensue. The phone rings, and Tom is summoned to take the call; Daisy goes after him, and the laconic, rather brittle Miss Baker, suddenly energized, jumps into the gossipy fray.

By the time the narrator, Nick, leaves the Buchanan home that evening, he describes himself as "a little disgusted." Which is exactly what the author wants the reader to feel.

The dialogue exchange below is taken from my novel *Caveat*, which opens in 1916. Notice how keeping diction and speech patterns consistent helps to establish the personality of each man, and their respective values. The first-person narrator here, Dr. Lucius Tipton (he of the Galloping Gallstones!), is speaking with Hank Beecham. Dr. Tipton is a convivial, educated man, but his speech is colloquial, and his grammar only loosely correct. Hank Beecham's diction, grammar, and pronunciation convey his limited formal education. Hank snaps off the ends and beginnings of words (and note when he cuts off the beginnings, I do use the apostrophe). Hank consistently says "would of" and "could of" rather than would have, could have.

This scene is the first time these characters have met after decades. Hank Beecham is a rainmaker, who has just that day returned to his hometown, St. Elmo, California, after twenty-some years away. The city fathers, desperate for rain during a long, crippling drought, have invited Hank, though the town in general has nothing but contempt for Hank's family. A fact Hank well knows. This evening scene takes place in the doctor's study. Hank met with the city fathers just that afternoon to set a price for his services. It's November 1916 and the Great War rages in Europe.

### RETURN OF THE NATIVE

"Well Hank, tell me how it is the city fathers gave up on God and turned to a rainmaker."

"Ask'em yourself. I take the job or I don't. I can say this though, the difference 'tween me and God is that God works for free."

"When He works," I offered.

"And when He don't, He can't be bought."

"You can?"

"I come dear. Fifty thousand. That's the wager I struck with them. All or nothing. I fill the reservoir, I get $50,000. I don't fill it and I don't get a penny."

It took me a bit to recover from the notion, much less the words, *fifty thousand dollars!* I'm not sure I did recover, but I managed to ask if he'd seen the reservoir yet. He hadn't. "You got a lot of confidence to make that kind of wager before you have a look."

"I'm good at what I do." Hank cracked his knuckles. "Fifty thousand," rolling the sum off his tongue as though it had flavor and succulence.

I opened a desk drawer and pulled out two cigars, offered one to Hank.

"I'm a cigarette man," he informed me.

"Cigarettes are nothing but a practice. Now, a good cigar—" I held it up to my ear and listened to it crinkle—"that's an art."

"I don't hold with art. Only science."

From behind my blazing match, I regarded this grizzled visitor whose intensity and conviction belied the emptiness of his blue eyes. "Well, I believe in science. Science always aspires to truth."

"Truth don't interest me, but I always held with science, even when I was fixing sewing machines. You seen one sewing machine, you seen 'em all, but a rainstorm, that's science. You get something new and glorious with every one. I stand there and the rain pours down on me and I know I done it. It's glorious, thunder and lightning wrestling over the sky. The wrath of it," he added, drawing out his bag of tobacco and papers, rolling a cigarette. "With science, I know what God must of felt like. If I held with God. Which I don't."

I took a bottle of Burning Bush Whiskey from the bottom drawer. "Can I offer you a drink?"

"I don't drink."

"I see." I burbled a little Burning Bush into a glass and remembered that his father Jeremiah Beecham drank, his brother too. "Well, you been spared your family's curse."

"Pa ruint everything he touched. 'Cept for me. I 'scaped 'cuz of Ma. Ma and luck."

"Luck's like rain," I said. "Sometimes it just comes and sometimes you got to make it yourself."

Hank Beecham snorted in what might once have been a laugh. "I made my luck all right, but it goes to show how there's no 'counting for how you come by it. My old man, he give me my luck. That blabbering drunken fool. He'd get so drunk he'd piss hisself 'fore he could get up off the chair—or the floor. But he give me ideas. Them and a lot a bruises, black eyes and a coupla cracked ribs now and then. It was the War the old man loved better than anything, 'cept drink. Shiloh, Missionary Ridge, all that smoke and bloodshed. The War was the happiest days of his life." Hank glanced at the Western Front headlines of the newspaper. "He'd of loved this war, too. It would of suited him."

Later in the book Hank's drunken father, Jeremiah, an embittered Confederate veteran, has a speech that is implied rather than outright quoted. (This is from a third-person narrator.)

Jeremiah could get teary on the subject of the immortal General Cleburne, the fightin'est Irishman who ever drew breath and the bravest and smartest general in the whole Confederate States of America. If Old Pat had been commander, he woulda saved the Confederacy, by God. Jeremiah would whup any scoundrel (*you jes name yer weapons, name 'em! Fists, knives*) who suggested that Grant was a greater general than Cleburne. Jeremiah spit on Grant. Sherman too. They never shoulda won at Shiloh. Why, that first day (to hear Jeremiah tell it) Sherman's men was so surprised they was bayoneted sleeping in their tents. And Grant? Grant had his back to the Tennessee River that first night and nowhere to go.

Grant shoulda drowned in the Tennessee River. Woulda drowned too, 'cept for . . .

Note that Jeremiah doesn't say "would of" or "could of." Jeremiah (older, addled, inebriate) says "woulda," and "coulda," and "shoulda." His diction is different than that of his son, his tone as well, and it's the tone that indicates character. Jeremiah is belligerent, spoiling for a fight. Hank speaks for the most part in short, clipped sentences that, taken collectively, convey the impression of an intense but wary man.

## Putting Dialogue on the Page

To make your dialogue effective, put it on the page correctly.

EACH SPEAKER GETS A NEW PARAGRAPH. The gestures, movements of each speaker should be kept in the same paragraph with her lines, and the whole of her speech kept together.

Example of form:

"So what do you think of my idea?" He stood in front of the drawing board, beaming. "Great, huh?"

"Interesting," was as much as I could offer. It was a good idea, but what would it matter? Jim had screwed his own chances, and I was the one who had to tell him. "You're an original, Jim."

"It'll go over great with the brass! Don't you think? Hey, they're going to love me!"

"Jim," I finally replied, cruelty being the better part of kindness in this case, "they're never going to love you. They caught you in the lie. You could right the Leaning Tower of Pisa, and it won't make up for the past."

Note in this exchange that *spoken dialogue* brackets both Jim's actions and the narrator's interior thought processes. Do this so that the next speaker can reply to something *immediate*. Note too that when Jim is identified by an action there in front of the drawing board, the narrative need not add *he said*. Clearly Jim said it because it's in his paragraph.

WEED OUT THE MERELY BANAL AND INEFFECTIVE. Never waste a half-page of valuable narrative real estate with the trivial:

"Hi."
"Hi."
"I'm Scarlett O'Hara."
"Hello, Scarlett. I'm Rhett Butler."
"How are you?"
"Oh, fine. How are you?"

This is all so predictable, so terribly boring your reader sleeps through it or simply doesn't read at all. This is equally true if you have dialogue conducted with too many one-liners. Do the trivial swiftly—"They greeted one other warmly"—and move along if that's all they're going to do.

BEWARE THE OVERUSE OF PROFANITY. While casual profanity might be a staple in the speech of your characters, on the page, like any-thing else, it carries more weight and can quickly become tedious, so much so that the reader's eyes just roll on past, and it becomes verbal wallpaper. In creating the speech of a young person, you might use "like" peppered through their dialogue, but again, having suggested its presence, do not overuse for the same reason.

BEWARE THE FREE-FLOATING "YA." Most people speak with an easy colloquial speech that the reader will absorb in an easy colloquial way. (See above with "Want go to the movies?" or "Wanna go to the movies?") If, in an effort to enforce the colloquial, you give your characters an untethered "ya," as in, "How ya doin'?" the *ya* calls needless attention to itself and distracts. It creates a "hard sound," as in the German affirmative, "ja" ( pronounced "yah"). To suggest casual context on the page, connect "ya" to other words. "Whaddaya think about that?" "Seeya!" In other constructions as well, you can combine words to create the flavor of speech. "Howzit hangin?" better suits this expression than "How is it hanging?" As noted above, these alterations have more significance in dialogue than they do in actual conversation.

ONLY QUOTE WHAT ACTUALLY PASSES PEOPLE'S LIPS. Do not quote thought processes. For those, simply say, she thought, or he considered, or he meditated. (In many nineteenth-century books interior thought is offered in quotes, but that practice has long since ended.) Often you don't even need, he thought, or mused. . . . Just above, as the narrator is speaking with Jim, just keeping the thoughts inside her head is sufficient. I would also caution against using italics to indicate thought process. Save italics for when you really want to rivet the reader's attention.

PAUSES IN REAL TIME SHOULD BE INDICATED WITHIN THE NARRATIVE ITSELF. He paused, looking out the window (then add dialogue). Or: She nibbled a long time at her thumbnail (then add dialogue). If your character is indecisive, hemming and hawing, use words to convey this: "I don't think we should go. I mean maybe it would be better just to, well I don't know . . . let's not, OK?" Stay away from *uh huh* and *uh uh*. Just as you doubtlessly did now, your reader must pause and think: is that uh huh, positive? Writers often use "Um . . ."to indicate polite or half-hearted demurral or even outright disagreement. Overuse of "Um . . ." makes your characters look dimwitted.

To pause, to lend weight or tension to a scene, you can (sparingly) add gestures and motions. As in:

"Will you take my case, Lawyer Abbot?"
Mr. Abbot poured more bourbon in the glass and regarded it
    philosophically before bolting it down in one gulp. "No, but
    I'll send you to someone who will."

(Notice that Lawyer Abbot does not frown and cough, harrumph, his eyebrows going up and down or otherwise facially carry on.)

ALL PUNCTUATION GOES INSIDE THE QUOTE MARKS. American usage uses double quotes. Punctuation can and should function as a writing tool. Yes! No! Yes? No? Each of these words is read completely differently. "Sonofabitch! You'd go without me!" has a whole different tone than "Sonofabitch, you'd go without me?" Other punctuation has special significance in rendering dialogue.

An ellipsis at the end of the sentence indicates that the speaker has *chosen* to let her words trail off. "Look, if only you'd try to see things my way, we could . . ."

A dash at the end of an uncompleted sentence indicates that the speaker has been interrupted involuntarily. "Look, if only you'd try to see things my way, we could—" (In which case, you must immediately supply the dialogue of the person butting in, or the action diverting attention.)

QUALIFYING ATTRIBUTIONS. Dialogue can be enhanced by vivid verbs that will contribute to the way in which it is spoken, and thus, the way it is read: wailed, scoffed, mourned, cackled, gloated, and so on. But beware of adverbs. Adverbs sprinkled among your attributions dilute. As in:

"I'd never do such a thing," he declared boldly.

To declare *is* bold. Change up to:

"I'd never do such a thing," he declared.

Better yet:

"I'd never do such a thing!" He glared at the others. "How could you even think that!"

The exclamation point *indicates* declaration. The outrage is enhanced with his glare, and the point is underscored with that final bit of dialogue using an exclamation point rather than a question mark.

## Adding Dialogue to Narrative

Early drafts of any prose work, fiction or memoir, tend to be heavy on narrative as you push forward. But when you go back (especially as you learn how to read like a writer in the revision chapter of this book!) you will see opportunities for expansion, to make scenic, to enrich what was merely descriptive. Often you can do that by adding dialogue.

Must your memoir have dialogue? Not necessarily. Richard Ford's laconic, loving portrait of his parents in *Between Them* has very little dialogue; his memoir is mostly conveyed in narrative in which he persistently refers to them rather formally as "my mother" and "my father." Narration unleavened with dialogue keeps things and people at a distance. Ford's parents are memorably portrayed, but without hearing their voices, they seem static to me, as though sitting for serene, sepia portraits. Even if dialogue is not your forte as a writer, work at it. Re-creating the voices you know, putting them on the page, will enliven your memoir.

## Prompt: Adding Dialogue

Take any material you have thus far created, and infuse it with dialogue. Let your people express themselves in speech patterns that are true to them.

Netta Gibbs took the last paragraph of "Saturday Night and Sunday Morning" and added dialogue. In doing so she also made it more scenic, giving her characters actions to accompany their dialogue.

> Joe and I could hear the ham slice hit the pan and the pancake batter sizzle on the griddle while Granny rattled on at Joe about being saved. Even then, she couldn't sit still. "When you gonna find Jesus, Joe? When you gonna let Him come into your life? Into your heart? I'm looking out for your own good, Joe, and I know Jesus would welcome you, all you have to do is just look up and say, Lord, I'm yours!"

"Well, Granny," Joe said, "I'm waiting to be called."

"Don't wait! Ask! Never mind. I'll ask." She raised her eyes and spatula to heaven. "Oh Lord, look down on this sweet soul, Joe Gibbs, find him, shower him with your love and the sure and certain knowledge of forgiveness for whatever he done, or whatever he might yet do. He knows he is a sinner, just like the rest of us, Lord, but . . ." She glanced over her shoulder at the stove. The pancakes were crisping up darker than she liked. She took them off, slid them on the plate, poked the ham with a fork, and handed the whole to Joe.

"Thanks, Granny. Got any eggs to go with this fine breakfast? You know just how I like them."

"I do," she said, cracking three of them in the grease the ham had left in the fry pan. She continued her conversation with the Lord, but she gave her attention to getting the eggs just the way Joe liked them.

Joe cut a piece of ham and smiled at me. He winked. I knew right then that he and I, angel and devil, youngest and oldest, were somehow united against all the rest of them, the whole family. The whole town for that matter. Maybe the whole world.

What do we know of Granny now that she has actually spoken? While she is a devout Christian, her hectoring is not fueled by hellfire, brimstone, or bitterness. After all, she makes no mention of Joe's having broken one of the Ten Commandments and spent eighteen months in the slammer for stealing a car. And we know she'll make sure his pancakes don't burn while she talks to the Lord on his behalf. Her character and her values are much more vivid. Joe, less so. What's given of him is terse, but his tone is respectful; he evades Granny's entreaties, but he doesn't disparage them.

## Did He Really Say That?

Frank McCourt is a great maestro of dialogue, even the rendering of an Irish schoolmaster's repetitive droning so that you, the reader, hear the drone, but you aren't stupefied into boredom. There are a few instances in *Angela's Ashes*, however, when the careful reader—which is to say a reader who is also a writer—might wonder at the content and placing of some of this exemplary dialogue.

Early on we meet a family named Clohessy who are even poorer and worse off than the McCourts; moreover there are more of them, seven boys and a girl. Paddy Clohessy is a school chum of Frankie's, and perhaps midway through the book the two boys play hooky together. That evening Frankie ends up at the Clohessy's miserable flat. Their living conditions are grotesque and given in gruesome detail. Mr. Clohessy lays dying of tuberculosis, and spewing up great ugly gobs of yellow goo into a bucket beside the bed. (The only bed in the flat.) On hearing that Frankie's mother was once Angela Sheehan, Mr. Clohessy brightens, waxes eloquent about what a fine dancer Angela was, how she and he had joyously danced in their youth. He asks Frankie to dance for him, right then and there, and though the boy protests he has no gift for it, Mr. Clohessy absolutely insists: if Frankie is Angela Sheehan's son, he surely must be able to dance. Frankie's attempts are both comic and pathetic. Darkness falls, and Frankie spends the night there on the floor with the other Clohessy children. He can't sleep, partially for the cold and also for the anxiety he knows his mother will be feeling (and he's never spent a night away from home). The following morning Angela with her youngest, a toddler, in tow, shows up, accompanied by the truant officer who, before he leaves, berates Frankie for making his mother worry. Denis Clohessy and Angela speak at loving and nostalgic length of their dancing days while Mr. Clohessy hacks and coughs and spews. He asks Angela to sing a song from their youth; Angela does her best, and Mr. Clohessy tries to sing with her but can't. Although Mrs. Clohessy and her seven children, plus the extra McCourt tot, are present, they fade or are faded into the narrative background so that no other sound, save for the song, are "heard." The reader does not have to know the song to recognize the pathos in Angela's voice. As that voice, those lyrics waft up off the page, some shimmer of the dancing Angela and Denis rises up in the reader's imagination as well.

Did Angela and Denis really say that? Did these long exchanges about their past actually transpire in the Clohessy's squalid flat? Were Mrs. Clohessy, her seven children, and the McCourt tot in fact hushed into silence? Did Angela truly sing a song and the dying man do his best to sing with her? Does it matter? Not to me. The memoir isn't written for the author to testify in court. It's written to evoke and portray the people in one's past, to give them authentic voices. This scene, this long exchange of dialogue gives us a glimpse of the youthful Angela Sheehan, the dancing girl, so very different from the beaten-down, impoverished woman we have thus far seen. Frank McCourt could have chosen to tell about his mother's youth in a brisk narrative, but would it have had the same veracity, the same vivacity, the same authenticity and emotional impact? Emphatically not. The author allowed their exchange to unspool, and shaped it to serve the past.

# 6 | The Family Story

*"Tell us a story," said the March Hare.*

*"Yes, please do," pleaded Alice . . .*

*"Once upon a time there were three little sisters," the Dormouse began*
*in a great hurry; "and their names were Elsie, Lacie and Tillie and they*
*lived at the bottom of a well—"*

*"What did they live on?" asked Alice who always took a great interest in*
*questions of eating and drinking.*

—Lewis Carroll, *Alice's Adventures in Wonderland*, 1865

Consider the family story. Every family has them. Every long-time friendship or bond of affection has them. Every profession has them, poets and painters and bakers and mechanics, teachers and preachers and doctors alike. Workplaces have them. Understand the term, then, in its loosest sense: any anecdote told over and over, smoothed, filed down by numerous tellings so the rough edges have been eroded away.

Often these sorts of stories end with an implied exclamation point; they are *funny!* They illuminate something funny ha-ha, funny peculiar, or touching.

Often they are told at the expense of the teller; that is, the teller or narrator of the story looks silly or callow or misguided, or perhaps merely naïve.

Or the family story might have no more merit than a remnant of how a certain thing came to be, or how a phrase has stuck, become part of the family lexicon, or part of a relationship.

Or they can be anecdotes that suggest a character trait or traits.

Or they might have an implied moral, a suggestion of take-heed; here's how I learned _____ whatever it was I learned.

These stories provide a kind "shorthand" among the people who tell them. More often than not, the people who share this story agree on it: yes, that's the way it happened. Sometimes the story has been so often rendered that different people within that family or cohort tell it with exactly the same vocal inflections.

A swift example of a lighthearted family story is The Beautiful Ham. In this anecdote I look silly, callow, and naïve. Here is the way I tell it.

THE BEAUTIFUL HAM

When I was nineteen I went home from college for Easter, and my mother had worked very hard putting together a great family meal. She lifted the ham out of the oven and said to me, "Isn't that a beautiful ham?" I, being a snotty and superior nineteen, replied that if I ever called a ham beautiful, I'd know my life was over and that I was dull as dishwater.

No doubt my mother felt shocked, hurt, and rebuked that I thought her dull as dishwater. But the *funny!* here is that once I became an adult, I loved to cook and in my lifetime, I have baked many a Beautiful Ham, and when I do, my mother never fails to comment on its beauty, and we laugh ourselves silly. The how-I-learned lesson inherent in the Beautiful Ham story? Do not be a snotty twit.

## The !!! versus The ???

Very often the family story will have a punch line, implied by the ! This is especially true of funny stories. While it had nothing to do with my family, I had a story I habitually told for laughs. In my youth I made a number of cross-country journeys, one in particular, driving a less-than-reliable car with a passenger, a friend who turned out to be a genuine liability. Over time I fashioned this harrowing journey so that the rough edges were smoothed, edited for amusement. I told it often, and I told it well with the !!! always collecting laughter. One day I told it to two writer friends. They did not laugh. I found this puzzling. They had a few pithy observations on the story, particularly on the friend who was a liability. Their reaction made me look behind the (artfully constructed) !!! and ask the ??? of my own experience. Altering the punctuation in an accepted story, I was obliged to delve, to ask fresh questions, to begin to build context outside of the tired, long-rehearsed telling, and retelling. In doing so, I looked more deeply, not only into the origins, but into the meaning. Inevitably, that story turned out to be longer. A lot longer. I revisited this anecdote in a novel. There are many amusing incidents in this novel, but chapter nineteen, the drive through the desert, is not one of them.

In my short memoir essay below, "Another Story," written to commemorate John Steinbeck's centennial, I tell a story about how my mother came to her great literary love, John Steinbeck. It has a ! a punch line that suggests the moral: do not cling to outdated prejudices. "Another Story" is the one my mother does not tell. This is the one with the question mark: *What did Steinbeck mean to you and why?* Asking the question invites introspection, possibly pain.

## ANOTHER STORY

This is not my story. I wasn't even there. But like a stone well worn, polished by the waters that run over it, this story has come to have a pleasing roundness in our family, the sharp edges, the pain buffed away. It is my mother's story, how she became a convert to John Steinbeck. She tells it well, as someone might recount discovering the True Faith. Like most converts, she is emphatic, vocal, eager to spread Steinbeck's Word. Her conversion story testifies to broadening your notions of what is relevant. Do not be narrow-minded: that's the implicit moral in the pain-free version. Like most such time-honed tales, the story itself can be reduced to a sort of punch line. The poignancy is in the context, always left unspoken in the telling.

The punch line goes something like this: In about 1969 my sister's high school home tutor required her to read *Cannery Row*. My sister Helen loved the novel, and she said to my mother, *You should read this book.* My mother said, *Oh no, I don't like Steinbeck.* And my sister replied, *What have you read of his that you don't like?* My mom was embarrassed to reply: *Nothing. I have never read a book by Steinbeck.*

As a girl growing up in Los Angeles in the 1930s, my mother, Peggy Kalpakian, had absorbed urban prejudices against the Okies pouring into California. Steinbeck of course was associated with them, and with other generally unsavory Not Nice people. But my mother agreed with Helen that this was an ancient, unthinking prejudice and so she read *Cannery Row.* Read *Tortilla Flat.* Read *Sweet Thursday.* These, the lighter, lively novels, first made a convert of her, though not yet a True Believer.

My mother moved from the charms of *Cannery Row* to *The Grapes of Wrath,* and *Mice and Men, In Dubious Battle,* on to the Shakespearean tapestry in *East of Eden.* As she waded further and deeper into Steinbeck's work and life, she quit getting the books from the library. She bought them all. Bought multiple copies. Pressed these extra copies into the hands of the indifferent, of unbelievers, saying, *Here is a book you will love. Read. Steinbeck is a wonderful writer.* But her conversion was not an altogether literary experience. John Steinbeck rescued my mother, as surely as if he, personally, placed his hand at her elbow and walked her through a dark time.

When she became a True Believer, I did not live there. I was 3,000 miles east of Southern California, in grad school, contributing my feet, my voice, my upraised arm to the protests, the antiwar marches in DC under the watchful eye of the National Guard.

My brother was 6,000 miles west of California. Vietnam. Serving in the US Army, Fourth Infantry. He was thrashing through jungles because he had cavalierly dropped a course at the community college, and once he was no longer a full-time student, he was ripe for the draft. His letters home from Vietnam were erratic, erratically received, erratically written, terrible, terrifying, and enigmatic. My parents despaired when the letters arrived. They despaired when there was silence. The mother of another boy in his unit (and they were boys, make no mistake, eighteen or nineteen) wrote a strange letter to my mom, advising her to "be strong." My mother did not reply. My parents woke each morning sick with unspeakable foreboding and went to bed each night sick with unspoken grief.

In this same year my parents trembled too at the prospect of losing their younger daughter. At seventeen, stalked by Crohn's disease, my sister Helen was too frail to go to school. She had undergone one massive surgery after another, none proving successful. She weighed less than ninety pounds. During the day, in addition to their ordinary jobs (my mother a secretary, my father a pharmaceutical rep), my parents bore these unshared, unbearable burdens. How can you tell the cheery neighbors, the supercilious boss, the client on whose business you rely, that you fear for your son's life, his health, his sanity? That you fear that your teenage daughter will die before she's twenty?

Into this daily vat of anxiety, dread, unexplained illness, the possibility of death in a distant jungle, there came into my mother's life the austere presence of John Steinbeck. Steinbeck's books, his vision, his characters, his prose spoke to her. Steinbeck stood beside my mother in the way old gods might have stood beside sufferers, save that my family's old gods had dissipated. Vanished. The Mormon faith that had sustained my father's people across the plains was certainly not my mother's faith (nor, by that time, my father's either). The Armenian Apostolic church that had sustained my mother's parents relied on a language she did not understand. The protestant faith of her youth seemed smug, unquestioning, unequal to the incipient tragedy that gnawed at her sleep and greeted her on waking. But Steinbeck was equal to the possibility of tragedy. Steinbeck recognized sorrow when he met it. He knew struggle. Steinbeck's rolling prose became a kind of Holy Writ.

Steinbeck's characters do not (to paraphrase Faulkner) prevail.

But they endure. And there are times when the enduring is sufficient. Indeed, when it is all that's possible, when the enduring itself bestows on suffering a kind of invisible nobility, which, in turn, creates courage. My mother—her life outwardly ordinary, middle class—found herself like Steinbeck's Okies, and like his beleaguered workers, like the limited Lennie, like farmers facing drought. She too was overwhelmed by forces she did not understand and could not control. Steinbeck's characters gave her the courage to endure. Beyond his books, Steinbeck's own life and personal struggles, his hard work, his self-doubt, all that spoke to her. When she read that his son had been in Vietnam, my mother knew that he understood. For years, John Steinbeck stood at her side. A grizzled ghost.

That he too was a Californian helped. Steinbeck's pastures of heaven were hers. He wrote of things and people, the light, the fields, the landscape, sensory experience my mother could easily picture, remember. His prose was not Shakespearean, shaped in arcane constructions; his sentences were hewn in California, beside the Pacific, in and of the long valleys. In the winters of my mother's discontent, dread, and anxiety, Steinbeck, his characters, his words, his evocations, his tragic vision came to my mother's rescue when she most needed rescue, when all else failed.

My brother certainly needed rescuing. One at a time she mailed Steinbeck's novels to him in Vietnam. Perhaps those books are still in Vietnam.

Young and full of my own endeavors, I did not need to be rescued, but she sent me the paperback novels too. I read them all. I was an enthusiast, but not a convert. For me (wishing even then, hoping to be a writer myself, but not yet brave enough to write) Steinbeck whispered that fiction could be created from the dust, the dry wind, the tumbleweed and oleander, from anonymous arroyos, the canyons of the California that I knew.

My sister got well. My brother came home from Vietnam. But that is another story.

## How-We-Came-to-Be Stories

Contented people do not uproot, repudiate their pasts, and move on. To leave one's home or homeland requires energy, strength, determination, or maybe just simple desperation. Somewhere in the past of most American families, such restless people existed, people who crossed frontiers of every sort. To cross the frontier in an American context suggests a confrontation with nature, venturing into unknowable dangers, unmapped places. To cross the European frontier suggests a confrontation with history, with language and identity: one shows one's papers, declares one's origins, crosses into another country, becomes foreign. Whether immigrants or pioneers, in their hearts and minds these discontented people carry their memories and music, their recipes, their religion, for some, their old languages. In short, they bear with them old identities that cannot be declared at customs, nor sloughed off from overburdened Conestogas rumbling west. Over time their remembered identities and adventures are gradually converted into narrative, family stories that refine difficult, even painful experience into the well-made, oft-told tale. These narratives become an anecdotal inheritance passed down to the generations that follow. Collectively these stories preserve family identity.

The impulse to trim and temper, smooth away the grim from family stories, tidying the past for children and grandchildren, is no doubt a sort of reflex. Conversely, there's the impulse to aggrandize, to make events wonderful and fantastic, to exaggerate the hardships endured or the costs extracted, to heighten the exploits. Whether these anecdotes are diminished or augmented, events elided, improved upon, or dramatically reshaped in the many times the stories are told, they achieve a kind of currency, shaped into the de facto truth. They are believed.

My father's people, the Johnsons, were Mormon pioneers scattered across Utah and Idaho, and later eastern Washington, a garrulous tribe with many such stories, told often and well. A reliable font of these stories was my dad's Aunt Lila. Lila Johnson Lutz (1905–1990) was an indomitable mother of seven, lively, delightful, energetic, profoundly religious, and utterly assured of her own correctness. In Lila's stories chronicling the Johnson family trials and triumphs—especially triumphs—the Johnsons always outsmart others, or enjoy some miraculous piece of good luck. The men are brilliant and just; the women are good wives and beloved mothers. There's no heartbreak, and no divorce. Everyone is devout. In listening to Aunt Lila recount Johnson family stories, you are to laugh when the story is funny, let your eyes grow wide when it concerns some prodigious feat, nod when it is poignant, but please do not ask stupid questions that will attempt to broaden that story beyond the narrative limits set by the teller, Lila Johnson Lutz. I learned this the hard way.

The urban Kalpakians, on the other hand, were not garrulous storytellers. My Armenian grandparents committed their past to silence. They sank their old country lives—war, genocide, deportations, broken families, unthinkable loss—into a silence so profound that the past was deprived of narrative oxygen, never articulated, until it gradually diminished into nothingness. With three exceptions. From all that was otherwise utterly unspeakable, my grandmother fashioned three charming stories. The Cup of Coffee Story! The Hot Water Tap Story! The Dumbell Story! Each was smoothed and shaped; each was purged of pain and told in exactly the same way with an exclamation point and an assuredly happy ending. I heard these three stories all my life. They were so ingrained in me that when I first tentatively picked up the pen to try to write fiction, I began with these, thinking cheerfully, well, at least I don't have to make up the stories! Here they are! I have only to put them on paper! (Speaking of silly, callow, misguided, naïve.) However, once I tried to turn each of these three stories into fiction, I inadvertently peeled back the !!! Obliged to create context for narrative, I asked questions of the past, and in doing so, I stared into an abyss of pain I had never guessed at.

Let's select just one of them. The Hot Water Tap Story! In my mother's *Centennial Memoir*, she describes this incident, which is set on Ellis Island, where the Kalpakians (the parents, Haroutune, and

Haigouhi; Haigouhi's younger brother, Haigauz; Peggy, the toddler; and her five-year-old sister) arrived after crossing the Mediterranean and the Atlantic from Constantinople (as it was known then). Peggy writes:

> We traveled 3rd Class, and our ship had mechanical problems in mid-Atlantic, and we were forced to stop for one full day till the repairs were complete. Because of this we arrived a little late at Ellis Island. The passengers disembarked 1st Class first, then 2nd Class, and by the time they got to 3rd class, *the quota had been filled.* So there we were on Ellis Island—in sight of New York City and the Statue of Liberty. We had arrived in America on August 2, 1923, which was the date of the funeral of President Warren G. Harding, who had died after a short illness. All of the federal offices were closed—including those on Ellis Island. All flags were at half mast. But our little family and Mom's younger brother, Haigauz, could not be processed in any event. The quota was filled and we had to get back on the ship (a Greek vessel) and go to Piraeus, Greece.
>
> Imagine the disappointment! Disappointment! Disappointment!
>
> Years later, when Mama told us about this Ellis Island experience, she mentioned only her great delight, surprise and astonishment at hot water coming out of the faucets!!!

There it is !!!! The Hot Water Story!!! Grandma, spellbound by the wonderful hot water pouring out of the tap!

Not a word escaped into the future about how they watched the disembarkation, first class, second class, coming finally to third class when the quota had been met. (A quota only just recently installed to keep in check the number of immigrants from Southern Europe.) Not a word about how they surely must have watched the 1923 Manhattan skyline, the Statue of Liberty in the near distance, knowing they would not set foot there. Nothing of the August heat baking against the heavy clothing they wore, my grandmother months into another pregnancy. Denied entry, their passport reads "deported," as though they had been accepted and then rejected. Usually those deemed unfit to enter the US were the elderly, the lame, the mad, the criminal, or the senile, but the Kalpakians were merely superfluous. Theirs was a one-way passport, no return trip to the Old Country, Turkey (and no wish to go back either). However, the steamship company had an agreement with the US government: the company must carry back to the point of origin anyone Immigration deemed unfit to enter. This was a Greek ship, returning to Greece, and the Kalpakians went back into the third-class hold. In my imagination I can all but see these five people lining up to reenter the ship (lining up along with the elderly, the lame, the mad, the criminal, or the senile who were also denied entry). I can imagine my mother, the toddler, fussing, wailing, having a tantrum in her father's arms. I can all but hear their footsteps clanging on the metal ramps leading back into the bowels of the ship, and the toddler's cries being swallowed up as they entered the dim-lit hold.

But that is my imagination because in the silence that surrounds my family's past, we *hear nothing*. No weeping, no gnashing, no swearing, no moaning, no wailing over their being deported, not a single curse, not a single word, not a single tear to register all that hope and effort and time and money expended into failure. Five people (five and a half if you count the daughter born in January 1924) deported back across the Atlantic, the Mediterranean, the Aegean, to Greece where they knew no one, and my grandmother had only schoolroom rudiments of the Greek language. The sole bit of this experience broken off, an anecdote torn, really, sheared of context and supplied with an exclamation point, was the Hot Water Tap Story! "Yes," my grandmother always used to say, her voice full of wonder, "I turned on the tap there at Ellis Island and out came hot water! Hot running water! Imagine that! I had never seen such a thing!"

Their passport is duly stamped on August 31, 1923, when they were provisionally admitted to Piraeus, Greece. They lived there (on what money, I know not; they were forbidden to take money out of Turkey) for two weeks before getting on yet another ship and making the crossings again, Aegean, Mediterranean, Atlantic, arriving in America this time in October 1923. That, too, is another story.

## Prompt: Revisiting the Well-Worn Past

Look among the family stories of your past. Identify a few of these stories and write up a straight version (the !!!). It will be swift, no doubt, like the Beautiful Ham, or exclaiming over the hot water, perhaps not much longer than your standard joke.

Now, use your imagination to ask questions of the past. Supply historical or contemporaneous context if you can. Peel back the !!! and replace it with a ??? Ask questions of the situation, the participants, the implied "moral" if there is one. Ask yourself, what is this story meant to suggest or illuminate? What is it meant to indicate about the teller (or the participants)? Perhaps most crucially, what is it meant to conceal? As is the case of the Hot Water Tap Story! which conceals crushing disappointment. Write another version, removing that laughter, that exclamation mark !!!

In doing so, step back from your material: where you may have written "my grandmother," or "my mother," or "my father"—in short, describing this person wholly in terms of their *relationship to you*, the narrator—use the name. What happens to the material when that person is rendered singularly, and not wholly shackled to you? For instance, when the Hot Water Tap Story! took place, 1923, my grandmother was certainly not my grandmother. She was twenty-two; she still had her old country name, Haigouhi. Reimagining, recasting that moment with my grandmother as *herself*, Haigouhi, changes the tenor of the experience.

> In the Ellis Island bathroom, Haigouhi stood before the sink. It had two chrome knobs. She turned the one and the sink suddenly steamed up under a rush of hot water. She jumped back when it burned her fingers. Hot water? How did they do that? How did

the water come out hot? Miraculous! Water poured into the sink, and steam wafted over the mirror hanging above, obscuring her youthful face, her sallow complexion, her mouth pinched, her eyes ringed with fatigue. Tentatively she turned the other knob and cold water poured into the sink. Haigouhi rolled up her sleeves and using both hands, she swirled the hot and the cold together, and the glorious warmth spread over her hands and she splashed her face, her hands again and again till the warmth of her tears mingled with the warmth of the water from the tap, and at last she wept, knowing they would be denied their destination, fearful of what lay ahead.

I've taken some imaginative liberties here. I am imagining a sink with two taps, not a single faucet where the hot and cold water automatically mingled, a small consideration perhaps, but I think historically correct for faucets in that era, and important for how she would have dealt with the water. I am imagining her tears, which seem to me justified, even though it must be said my grandmother was not the sort to cry, ever, or for any reason. (When my grandfather died in 1963, she alone stood tearless at his graveside.) But here, Ellis Island, 1923, she is not a stoic grandmother. She is Haigouhi, a young woman, mother of two, several months pregnant with a third child, in circumstances that have tested her courage and broken her heart. From a writerly perspective, placing Haigouhi herself as the point-of-view renders the Hot Water Tap Story! immediate, experiential, and not simply a tired, oft-repeated tale. Indeed, were I to recast with the verbs in present tense (Haigouhi stands before the sink. It has two chrome knobs. She turns the one and the sink suddenly steams up . . . ), that would make it even more immediate.

In 1992 I was on a book tour for my novel *Graced Land* (yes, this is back in the day when they used to do that) traveling from where to where, I can't remember, but I was going through the Chicago airport. The O'Hare Airport had been recently renovated, or perhaps it was a wholly new terminal; in any event, it was dazzling with bright arcs of rainbow-colored lights darting over fantastically high ceilings that suggested stained glass in a traveler's cathedral. I walked down these vast halls, and finally I found my gate and before the plane boarded, I went into the bathroom. Amid the usual clang of stall doors, the flush of toilets, and the harsh florescent light, I stood there at the sink, befuddled. Where were the taps? How could I turn on the faucet? I glanced to the side and saw a woman wave her hands, low in the sink. Tentatively I did the same, waved my hands under the faucet, and Behold! Water came gushing out, warm water! I was surprised! How did they do that? And then I started to laugh out loud, wishing my grandmother were still alive so I could tell her how I recognized the truth of her story, yes, even amid the "Disappointment, disappointment, disappointment!" there it was: hot water for the weary, delighted traveler.

———

In revising the family story, applaud yourself for insight and courage to look beyond or behind the merely acceptable, to write a new version of the heretofore unquestioned. However, relatives who read your revised, expanded family story, the !!! removed and replaced with ??? may, like Aunt Lila, not like it very much. You will have upended the telling, perhaps altered the narrative voice, and very likely brought forth the inconvenient or unhappy (like the role of John Steinbeck in my mother's life). Do not fret the familial ire. It will pass. Anyone who objects to your revision will finally ignore it. Family stories are utterly indestructible. No matter what you, the writer, do to them, they have the narrative equivalent of the shelf life of Twinkies, or peppermint candies at Christmas, or boxed macaroni and cheese. They last forever.

# 7 | Past and Present

*The past is a foreign country; they do things differently there.*
—L. P. Hartley, *The Go-Between*, 1953


The past was once the present. And when it was the present, it was a jumble of possibility and routine, a gumbo of obligation and necessity, a muddle of anxiety and pleasure, a patchwork of setbacks and rewards, unrealized hopes, unjustified fears. We commemorate the big, obvious moments—graduations, weddings, the birth of a child, the death of someone beloved—but the days that were actually significant slide by seemingly without import or impact. We live through important milestones with scant awareness of their significance. Think of the day you first met the person you married (or loved and didn't marry). Or the day you first met the person who became your best friend. Did the heavens part? Did the Hallelujah chorus tune up? When I first met the man I eventually married, it was at the swimming pool of the apartment complex where we both lived, a casual introduction on a very ordinary day. If I had kept a journal in those years (which I did not) I would not even have mentioned meeting him. And yet, clearly, that was a crucial day in my life. Many years later there was a party I didn't want to go to. My mother insisted I go; she came over to babysit so I could, and there I met a woman who became my best friend. The days that I met these important people— the man I married and the friend I cherished—were part of a pattern only ascertained, only visible once that present had become the past.

The memoir always has the advantage of hindsight. It recognizes the significance of people and events. Memoir pulls the *past into a pattern*. The experience described in the memoir is not fresh. Not raw. The grit of daily life has been expunged, washed away. The memoir is a narrative crafted and made coherent.

Journals, diaries, and letters—what historians call primary documents—are literary forms contemporaneous with the events themselves. They do not have the perspective of hindsight to discern significance. Take for instance the journals of Dorothy Wordsworth (1771–1855), who shared her adult life with her brother, poet William Wordsworth. Her copious journals provide a description of their day-to-day lives and provide readers with foundational insights into the work of Wordsworth, Coleridge, and the other writers of England's Lake District in the early nineteenth century. In 1897, some forty years after her death, Dorothy Wordsworth's journals were edited and published. The editor of that 1897 edition assured his readers that *nothing of any literary value* had been excised. One particular day in 1802 is especially fascinating. On this day Dorothy noted that William began work on his famous "Immortality Ode . . ." and then brother and sister "sat in the orchard." The reader thus imagines Dorothy and William poetically among the apple trees while William reads aloud what he had written that day. But what about that ellipsis . . . ? It indicates that *something* has been edited out. But what? John Worthen filled in that ellipsis in his 2001 book, *The Gang: Coleridge, the Hutchinsons & the Wordsworths in 1802.* Reading Dorothy's original diaries, Worthen found that on that particular day, after William began the "Immortality Ode," a Mr. Oliff delivered a load of dung, and William went off to spread that dung in the garden. *Then* they sat in the orchard. The 1897 editor saw the manure (the grit of daily life) of no literary value whatsoever, so he expunged it with an ellipsis. But in 1802, *as that day was lived*, the immortal and the manure were all mixed up.

In the diary and the letter as literary forms, the present is, so to speak, unwashed. As a result, diaries and letters have a raw vitality to them. They are based in immediacy, not based in memory. As literary forms they have different demands, delights, and limitations.

DIARY OR JOURNAL: The intended reader of a diary or a journal is oneself. Thus there's no need for the writer to add context or significance or identify individuals, places, emotions. A diary is fresh, raw, written at the moment, without hindsight, the crucial and important larded in (usually unknowingly) with the trivial. Indeed, the diary or journal can be written in cipher known only to the person who holds the pen.

LETTER: The intended reader of a letter is someone outside the self, but an individual with built-in context and some connection to the writer. (Or why would they be writing a letter?) A letter, too, is written without hindsight, the crucial and important larded in with the trivial. It too has the freshness of contemporary events on it, the surprise and delight (or despair) of day-to-day life, rendered often without self-consciousness. Not as intimate as the journal, the letter presupposes an outside reader, but one allied to the writer.

MEMOIR: The intended reader of the memoir is someone altogether outside of the writer, outside of the writer's immediate context, indeed, even unknown to the writer. For this reader, the writer *must* give context and character, delineate and expand, create connections, offer introductions and explanatory observations. The memoir gives the past shape and meaning that it did not have when it was the present. It clothes the past in structure, dresses it up in narrative. The past has been edited for cohesion and significance.

When I was about eleven, I was given a gift of a little five-year diary (each day was allotted four lines for each of the five years) with a lock. With no regard for the neat constrictions of four lines, I sometimes filled up whole pages for one day. This diary was salvaged amid the boxes of family memorabilia inundated with water when our basement flooded. Reading it later, how vividly memory sprang to life! Incidents and people I had entirely forgotten jumped off the page, never mind the clumsy, childish scrawl. Though I noted some fears (my little sister was very ill), mine was not an introspective diary. In truth, my childhood diary, though not at all pious, was rather like Anna Green

Winslow's 1771 diary in that it was full of trivial incidents, "Went for ice cream . . ." and the like. Also among the material rescued from the flooded basement, there was an endearing expense diary my mother kept in 1940. She was just out of high school and working at her first job where she was paid $16.50 a week, a little more than minimum wage, which at the time was 40 cents an hour. Miss Peggy Kalpakian kept careful notes and expenditures, including the purchase of *The Saturday Evening Post* (5 cents) and a 2-cent donation to charity. Even then, her checkbook always balanced.

Personal letters don't usually chronicle such minute notations. A letter communicates to a reader outside the self, so presumably the writer has something to say. The tone in which the letter is written will often convey something of the writer's mood, or the reader's expectations, as well as the relationship between the reader and the writer. One of the most profound experiences of my reading life was the superbly edited *The Children of Pride* (1973). The book laid out chronologically the letters exchanged among a vast tribe of a wealthy Georgia family from 1854 to 1868. As these people lived through events leading to the Civil War, the war itself, and its aftermath, their voices created a sort of opera across eighteen-hundred-some-odd pages.

Published volumes of collected letters or diaries offer compelling, sometimes surprising insight to people we have come to admire. In the many volumes of her collected letters, and in her diaries, I found it disconcerting to read how often Virginia Woolf bemoans the Servant Problem. If the Great Virginia had written a memoir, she probably would not have included being persistently vexed with the servants; yet, here are her immediate, everyday household dilemmas. In *The Correspondence of F. Scott Fitzgerald*, particularly in the 1930s Scott whines constantly about money and brags about how long he has been on the wagon, a sad portrait of his state of mind, his situation. (*The Crack-Up*, personal essays he published in *Esquire* in the 1930s are, to me, less memoirs and more a forty-year-old man putting his twenty-year-old self under intense, unflattering scrutiny.)

If you are fortunate enough to have journals and letters at hand as you write a memoir, consider them a resource. They can provide you with that vivid glimpse of the past when it was the present. They have about them the ring of the genuine, the unvarnished. They are unleavened by perspective. But beware how you use them. Letters and journals cannot simply be plopped down into the pages of your memoir and left to stand untended. In using diaries and letters, you might well winnow out the inconsequential (the delivery of dung) and highlight the memorable and dramatic (the early stages of a poem). You will be obliged to fill in, enlarge upon, detail for the reader, what the diarist or the letter writer had no need to address or include. In weaving your diaries, journals, and letters into your memoir, it's not enough to say, "My journal for that day notes . . ." or simply to set down large tracts of info quoted from your journals. Take from these sources, the specificity, the granular, the sense of the immediate to enrich your tale, but remember that you are author of a *memoir*. The memoir relies upon perspective to filter raw experience, to select, to sift, to shape. You will need to supply what the diarist will not.

And what might that be? Well, scenic depiction for one. The writer of the journal would probably not evoke the scenic particulars of her environment, material crucial to the memoir. (Dorothy Wordsworth does not describe the orchard.) Along those same lines, the diarist probably wouldn't include descriptions of the individuals who people her pages, nor would she supply character development for them. Dorothy would not identify them, as say, my brother, William Wordsworth. The diary, the letter might offer vivid accounts of bad moods, bad moves, petty annoyances, states of outrage, as well as giddy happiness, perhaps even unflattering names cast upon annoying people, but none of that suffices for character development. People might float in and out of the diary with no clear indication of who is important—and who is not, like Mr. Oliff who brought the dung. Plunged into and hemmed in by the immediate, the diary and the letter would not offer the reader backgrounds or transitions that are so essential to the memoir. In short, individuals and events are untethered from significant contexts.

You can see all this at work in the following materials—a diary entry, a letter, and a small portion of a memoir all written by the same woman, Ginny Brothers Doyle, a former rodeo star-turned-stuntwoman in the 1950s and '60s. The journal, the letter, and the portion of the memoir all chronicle the same events, but look how very different they are! The journal and the letter are written contemporaneous with the events when Ginny was on location up in the mountains, shooting scenes for a 1954 Western called *Gold of the Yukon*. The memoir, *Fifty Years a Cowgirl*, published some forty-five years later, chronicled her rodeo life and film career, including *Gold of the Yukon*.

### DIARY

*Feb. 17 1954.* Les horse slipped on ice. Went down & Les thrown into the river. Those bastards just kept filming. Horse cd not get up. Les went for our gun. Out of it's misery, poor beast. Left it there in the river. Too cold to shower. Food is swill. Poker −$20 / Auggie. + $5 / Johnny Farr+ $10 / 3 days down. 4 to go in this location hell.

Ginny offers no context here. Les is her stuntman husband. Does she say that? Of course not. Who are Auggie and Johnny Farr? She knows; we don't. She will be the only reader, so no respect for spelling, grammar, or syntax, or even, for that matter, clarity.

### LETTER

*Feb. 18 1954*
Dear Ma
    They told us this Gold of the Yukon would be an EZ shoot, and Grayson's Lodge would be a picnic location. They call it rustic. I call it butt-numbing. I'm sure it's saving the producer a lot of green. Me & Les have to share a room with Auggie & Frances & that kid Troy. What a Twit, 5 lines & he thinks he's Gary Cooper. At least Troy can sort of ride a horse. More than can be said for Lois Bonner. They had to rewrite her lines on set so she wd. not have say them on horseback. She cd. not act her way of out a paper bag. She's screwing Inscore, of course. I got tales for you when I get

home, but not enuf time here to rattle on. Anyway, Ma, Troy snores like Steamboat Willie so none of us get any sleep. & it's so damned cold, I have to put my nose in Les's armpit just to keep it warm. At least there's a fireplace there in the big main room downstairs where we play cards & have meals. They're feeding us swill, greasy stews with big chunks of onion & potato still hard in the middle. It's so damned cold that when the long skirt I have to wear gets all wet at the hem, it freezes. How am I sposed do a running jump like that? Skirt's so heavy by the third take, I can hardly get on & off the horse. Inscore has us out there at freezing dawn, & re-shoot at dusk. For the light for the light! he says. The light is more important to him than the crew or the animals. We lost a horse to the river, Ma. It slipped on ice, some frozen slime, went down, throwing Les into the water where he about froze before he waded out. The horse couldn't get up. Broken leg. Inscore kept shouting at the cameraman, Keep shooting! Keep shooting! Never mind the fucking horse! But we, all of us, we were done for the day, by god, & that bastard cd roll those cameras to hell & back, wasn't none of us going to move for Eugene Inscore. Les went to our car, got his pistol, and brot it back. Inscore shut up then. Oh yes, bet your life he did. He probably thought Les was going to shoot him. But Les gave that poor suffering beast two quick ones to the head. Les took it real hard. Drank half a bottle of bourbon before he could sleep at all. I won $5 in a poker game from Johnny Farr. Yes, Ma, he's handsome, but dumb as sheep. Will you call Doris give me a haircut appt next Monday? I know you hate my hair cut so short, but I have to wear these damned wigs so I look like Lois Bonner. Ha ha ha. Well gotta go. Don't worry about me. I am just as happy as if I had sense.

LOVE FROM BOTH OF US.
*Ginny*

Again the style is intimate. Ginny cares nothing for spelling, or grammar, or paragraphing; she doesn't use quote marks; she drops words and doesn't correct; and she uses quickie spelling and symbols. But since this is written for a reader outside herself, she is obliged to offer more context than she did in her diary entry. Still, she doesn't identify Inscore as the director; Ma would know this. The drama of the horse slipping on ice, breaking its leg, and having to be shot, that terrible scene is larded in with the five bucks she won in a poker game from the leading man, handsome Johnny Farr. (Though she doesn't identify him as the leading man; Ma would know that too.)

These same events come to the public in a very different way in the memoir Ginny later published. The past has been sifted for significance. Time (forty-five years) has altered some of that significance. Also, and equally important, she is writing for a reader unknown to her.

EXCERPT FROM *FIFTY YEARS A COWGIRL*,
A MEMOIR BY STUNTWOMAN VIRGINIA DOYLE,
PUBLISHED IN 1999

I performed Lois Bonner's stunts for a TV series, and three motion pictures. The best known of course, was the classic Western, *Gold of the Yukon* also starring Johnny Farr and Carson Summers as the two greedy brothers. Lois Bonner played the Girl. Like most young actresses, Lois Bonner could not ride a horse, but naturally, to get the part, she told the director that she could. Les tried to teach her, just like he had taught many others, but Miss Bonner was one of his failures. She was too scared to sit on a horse. She didn't even like to be around them. So in the film I would tear across the snow on horseback, rein the horse in, and jump off, my nose would be dripping with the cold, my face red and raw. In the next shot without a hair out of place, her face barely pink, there was Lois Bonner. She was a fine actress and her tragic death saddened everyone who knew her.

I believe that *Gold of the Yukon* was her first motion picture. It the only picture I ever made with the famous director, Eugene Inscore, and being part of it was one of the highlights of my career. Inscore was perfectionist. On the week-long location shoot at Grayson's Lodge, the big stars, Johnny Farr and Lois Bonner and Carson Summers had life easy compared to the crew, and especially the stunt riders. Sometimes Mr. Inscore would have us on horseback from early morning to near dusk hoping to get the light just right. He was a real tyrant on the set, but afterwards, he would make jokes and play cards with the cast and crew. Grayson's Lodge (since burned down) had a big fireplace in the main room, but the bedrooms were very cold and the food was terrible. Mr. Inscore kept telling us we were suffering for our art. When *Gold of the Yukon* won the Oscar in 1955, he had a dozen roses sent to every last person who worked on the film, including the stunt riders, the makeup people, costumes, props. Everyone. He was a real gentleman. *Gold of the Yukon* was Troy Ellis's first picture and though he had only a few lines, everyone could see immediately he was star material.

Clearly, in the memoir, the ease, the candor of the lingo of the more private communications, the diary and letter, are now replaced by an entirely different, more formal tone. The narrator's experience is cast in measured though not brilliant prose, but certainly correctly, grammatically rendered. Events discussed in the memoir are given in a different light, and with different emphasis, altered presentation for public consumption. The passage of time has given people and events a perspective Ginny did not have in 1954. The picture, *Gold of the Yukon*, though it may have been hell to film, won an Oscar, which means it was an important event in the careers of everyone associated with it. Troy, the twit actor who, with five lines to speak, thought he was Gary Cooper, in fact became a big star. Perhaps Mr. Inscore became such a big shot that calling him anything less than "a real gentleman" would be imprudent. Though his tyranny on set is noted, it's softened by his playing cards and making jokes and sending roses to the cast and crew. His affair with Lois Bonner goes unmentioned. Lois apparently died under tragic circumstances, and though Ginny relates the story of her inability to speak lines from horseback, it's given here blandly, without the good-natured contempt of Ginny's letter. The bad food, the cold, the hardships the entire crew faced while on location, she mentions these. But the shooting of the horse? Of the horse that slipped on ice, fell, broke its leg, and threw Les into the icy water; of the director screaming at the cameraman to go on filming even though the injured animal lay there suffering; of Les going to his car, getting a pistol, and shooting the horse twice in the head? Not a word.

The past is a foreign country; they do things differently there.

_____

## Prompt: Re-Creating Immediacy

Take a character, not yourself, the narrator, but another character from your memoir and recast the experience you have described as a *journal* or *diary* entry that a person would write. Remember that a diary, written for the self, can be oblique, hurried, even unclear.

Second, cast that experience as a *letter* written to whomever. A letter will aspire to some higher degree of clarity than the diary entry. The letter will also reflect the degree of intimacy the writer and reader share.

In doing so, remember how these people expressed themselves when you were writing their dialogue. Bring that same vivacity to the letter and the journal. Correct grammar, correct spelling are not essential. Also remember that the journal and the letter lack perspective, and that the significant and trivial can lay side by side, the writer not, at that point, knowing the difference.

Write. Walk away. Return later and ask yourself: in moving more closely to this individual, to what they thought, felt *at the moment*, have you brought some new insight to that person's experience? To your own understanding of their emotions, or their point of view? Are you, the writer, better able to imagine the past when it was the present?

# 8 | The Madding Crowd

*A large cask of wine had been dropped and broken, in the street.... A shrill sound of laughter and of amused voices—voices of men, women, and children—resounded... while this wine game lasted. There was little roughness in the sport, and much playfulness... special companionship ... especially among the luckier or lighter-hearted, to frolicsome embraces, drinking of healths, shaking of hands, and even joining of hands and dancing, a dozen together.*
—Charles Dickens, *A Tale of Two Cities*

Though life's intimate moments are the most memorable, the crowded moments are the most numerous. From the time you go to school and learn to stand in line, you learn to live in crowds. Even in the nuclear family, if you were child number three or four, you were born into a crowd scene. For the writer, basically, any situation in which there are more than three or four people constitutes a crowd scene. To render crowds vividly, the writer must move many, sometimes disparate, characters through a landscape, balance the voices of major and minor players, create the mood surrounding the event, and attribute dialogue as needed—oh, and not leave the reader confused. A well-done crowd scene, challenging as it is, can root your characters in their social milieu and portray vivid backgrounds.

*There were a lot of people there and they were all making noise.* Even for the most devoted minimalist, such a sentence fails. How, as a writer, to navigate the madding crowd?

Basically, in narrative prose there are four major tactics a writer can use to create compelling crowd scenes. Not all of these four can be easily invoked by the memoir writer who is tied to a first-person narrator, but I offer them all nonetheless.

## The Implicated Narrator

The Implicated Narrator is picked up in the tide of the events. The guy in the mosh pit at the rock concert, the solider on the battlefield, the protestor running from tear gas, or even simply someone drinking too much at a cocktail party, this narrator partakes of the mood or the perils or the pleasures of that crowd. These pleasures or perils may impinge upon, even impugn the narrator's vision, judgment.

In the scene below, the Implicated Narrator, Cilla Jackson, is about fourteen, and her little sister, Lisa Marie, is about eight. Cilla absorbs the all-round high everywhere rampant, especially after she and her little sister are discovered and whisked into the living room. The occasion is late one Saturday night in 1982 when her mother, Joyce has bought a used Studebaker that has sentimental significance for her, and she and a few friends have just towed it into the garage.

### THE RESURRECTION AND THE LIFE OF THE PARTY

I lie there in bed, and listen to all four of them come into the living room, flop down, and say with one voice they're so beat, they're going to die.

Then one of these near dead, I don't know which one, gets up and goes to the stereo and on comes Jailhouse Rock, and with that—I am here to tell you—comes the Resurrection and the Life of the party. Elvis's early stuff, fast, hard, alive, those songs that your feet can't stand, music that downright carbonates your toes and even if you didn't want to get up and dance, your feet would just desert you and go-man-go by themselves. Lisa wakes up and rubs her eyes. We get up out of bed, and go crouch down in the hall and watch everything through the heater grate in the wall. The phone's ringing off the hook and there's car doors slamming and chairs scraping back and the snap of pop-tops and the sewing machine gets pushed against the wall and the squeal of protest the ironing board makes when it comes down. There's Dogleg and Stan and

Mama and Sandee, of course, and Charleen and her new husband, and Phil and his new girlfriend. And there's a bunch of others we don't even know. The music pumps up and everyone in the living room is all shook up and dancing the shake-down-shimmy. You can feel it vibrating the heater grate, and if you was deaf, you'd know there was dancing and happiness. You'd know grief had flown out the window.

Me and Lisa look at one another, smiling. I whisper, "There hasn't been music or laughing like that in this house since dad left us and Elvis died."

The hall door opens fast and it's Uncle Phil, and he laughs out loud, "Well, lookee here! A couple of sweet girls! Come on, girls!"

We sing, right along, dance along with Mama and Sandee, with all of them. One by one, the guys from my uncle's band show up. They didn't any of them bring their instruments, but they brought their feet and they are all dancing with anything that will move and some that won't. Dogleg's got hold of the ironing board, pulled it up close to him, making it promise not to step on his Blue Suede Shoes. . . . My uncle Stan picks up a couple of clothes hangers and beats on the upright piano, and Dogleg flips that piano open. Stan and Dogleg, they play backup for Elvis like he is right here with us, singing in this very room.

Dancing, hands held over their heads and beers held high, a whole lot of shaking going on. The thump of feet, the cry and shout . . . laughter like it was just ripped out of the walls, like lathe-and-plaster turned to laugh and plaster, joint jumping, all our Elvis pictures, even that big, framed King Creole on the wall, bouncing like the King was happy at last to hear us happy. There was thunder in the floor and I felt his presence here with us, and I knew right then, there was no tomb that could hold Elvis or his music. Well, there was thunder at the door too, but it was the cops.

The classic Implicated Narrator is Nick Carraway in *The Great Gatsby*. This novel is cast as Nick's memoir of the summer of 1922 when he rented a house near the fabulous mansion of Jay Gatsby. Much, even most, of the story is conveyed through crowd scenes, parties at Gatsby's, or other social situations.

At the first Gatsby party, Nick, knowing no one, meanders through the crowd looking for his host. As he wanders he characterizes the other guests who are mostly nameless and without backgrounds, who are literally *characterized* by their clothes, attitude, or antics. As the evening continues, and the festivities accelerate, Nick, who is drinking but not altogether drunk, circles back around to many of these characters, touches on them, especially as the liquor flows and they become more drunk, more boisterous, or tearful. Finally, near dawn, Nick, now fairly drunk, stumbles home where he witnesses the auto accident that foreshadows the end of the novel.

After establishing this first party in glorious detail, to give the *sense* of the rest of Gatsby's parties that summer (and so that the author can evoke them without the need to chronicle each), Nick, the narrator, shares with the reader a long list of the *names*, scribbled on the back of a train timetable, various people who attended these galas over the course of the summer. They are not characters, just (often funny) names. It's a brilliant, tactically economical effect.

## The Onlooker

The Onlooker can be, and usually is, a more thoughtful, ruminative narrator. This narrator is often at some distance from the crowd, whether that is physical distance or mental distance. The Onlooker can be ironic, even judgmental, because they are not part of the action. The narrator circulates through the crowd, or watches from a distance, giving sharp unsentimental descriptions. (A great illustration of the Onlooker is in Joni Mitchell's song, "People's Parties.")

In the selection below, from my story "The Delinquent Virgin," the Onlooker, Reverend Reedy, is clueless, even a little stunned, and certainly not part of the general hubbub around him. Though this story is told in third person, the point of view is rooted in the consciousness of Reverend Hamilton Reedy, the pastor of a well-to-do congregation. Reverend Reedy has just arrived at the St. Elmo police station to collect some goods stolen from the church and recovered by the cops (though the thief remains unknown).

## THE COP SHOP

The downtown police station was crowded this evening and Hamilton was told to take a number while the duty officers processed those before him. The Reverend Reedy tried to remember the last time he had been called by a number. Perhaps at the Cake Box Bakery on the day before Thanksgiving—last year, or perhaps the year before. Here, he sat on a bench amid the sorts of people he almost never saw, and watched as police processed half a dozen kids arrested for shoplifting. The kids wore pants so huge they each looked like full sail clipperships and from the cargo holds of these ships there issued forth an astonishing array of stolen goods, including four videos from the boxer shorts of a boy who had refused to sit down. He had also refused to shut up. With his compatriots he spat and smirked and swore. All the gang members addressed one another and the cops—indeed everyone present, male or female—as *puta*, whore, bitch, fucker, inviting them to suck various substances and informing them they all sucked in general. Their oaths counterpointed the yelps of a dreadlocked, gray-bearded veteran wearing a VFW denim jacket who sat next to Hamilton. The veteran alternately protested and wept about a chain of human ears. At least that's what Reedy thought he said. The veteran was being charged with disturbing the peace, assault and public nuisance. He didn't seem to care; he begged Reedy to look at the chain of human ears he wore around his neck. There was no such chain. There was nothing.

All this clattered against the ring of phones, the blip and natter of computers, the clank of handcuffs. Suddenly the waiting room split with the screech of a woman in a short dress and running shoes, dragged in by two armed officers while she clutched at, refused to relinquish the handle of a baby carriage. She screamed that she wasn't going to steal the baby, just talk to it. To Hamilton's horror, as she wrestled with the cops, the baby carriage overturned and garbage bags with her belongings tumbled out, as did a doll, a baby doll warmly clad in soiled jammies who bleated out a weak, *Maaa-Maaa, Maaa-Maaa.*

"Next! Number 56!" cried out the duty officer. "Number 56! Where are you?"

Hamilton eagerly rose and went to the desk.

A sophisticated use of the Onlooker is in the classic American novel *To Kill a Mockingbird,* which is also cast as a memoir; the first-person narrator, Scout, relates events of her childhood. In Chapter 15, Atticus and the sheriff are afraid a mob will come after Tom Robinson, forcibly take him from the jail, and lynch him. Atticus and the sheriff take turns guarding the jailhouse door all night long. Though Scout and Jem have been told to stay at home, they disobey their father. They go to the jail and hide in the bushes out of sight, watching while their father sits reading under the light that hangs over the door. Suddenly cars and trucks drive up and disgorge a lot of men who are not at all differentiated, who in fact are visually *kept in shadow,* though (oddly) Scout tells us she and Jem are close enough to smell them. As Onlookers the children listen to the angry exchanges between Atticus and the mob. Suddenly Scout bolts toward her father and though the crowd remains mostly in darkness, she singles out Mr. Cunningham. She calls out to him, asking after his boy. Slowly, even shamefully, the men disperse.

The scene is masterfully done, though not told with any irony or particular judgment or even fear. Though the reader knows what the mob intended, Scout seemingly does not.

## The View From

The View From, an aerial sweep, is more easily accomplished with a third person narrator. The View From is a good tactic to use when you want to invoke the general sense of the crowd (or the environment) without developing any single character.

Your first-person narrator need not be absolutely shackled to the ground, especially if you use The View From as an opener to establish the mood and tenor, the ambience of the crowd. The narrator can, say, stand at the top of stairs, or from a window and look down and out and over the scene. In the memoir you can use The View From imaginatively, as Dickens does below in the first stave of *A Christmas Carol*. There is no central figure here, only a narrative voice flitting overhead, darting among the London streets, alighting on scenes and people, the highest to the lowest—the working men in front of the brazier, the shop windows, the Lord Mayor's house, the tailor's meager dwelling—on Christmas Eve. Developing none of them, but evoking the crowd and the spirit of the crowd.

CHRISTMAS EVE

Meanwhile the fog and darkness thickened so, that people ran about with flaring links, proffering their services to go before horses in carriages, and conduct them on their way. The ancient tower of a church, whose gruff old bell was always peeping slily down at Scrooge out of a Gothic window in the wall, became invisible, and struck the hours and quarters in the clouds, with tremulous vibrations afterwards as if its teeth were chattering in its frozen head up there. The cold became intense. In the main street at the corner of the court, some labourers were repairing the gas-pipes, and had lighted a great fire in a brazier, round which a party of ragged men and boys were gathered: warming their hands and winking their eyes before the blaze in rapture. The water-plug being left in solitude, its overflowing sullenly congealed, and turned to misanthropic ice. The brightness of the shops where holly sprigs and berries crackled in the lamp heat of the windows, made pale faces ruddy as they passed. Poulterers' and grocers' trades became a splendid joke; a glorious pageant, with which it was next to impossible to believe that such dull principles as bargain and sale had anything to do. The Lord Mayor, in the stronghold of the mighty Mansion House, gave orders to his fifty cooks and butlers to keep Christmas as a Lord Mayor's household should; and even the little tailor, whom he had fined five shillings on the previous Monday for being drunk and bloodthirsty in the streets, stirred up to-morrow's pudding in his garret, while his lean wife and the baby sallied out to buy the beef.

The light and bright communal bustle conveyed here will contrast vividly with the grim, dark, tomb-like silence of Scrooge's lonely bedchamber where the rest of the story will take place.

## The Relay Team

In this technique characters can come upon one another, linger there, and then "pass the baton" as the narrative follows the next character, their experience, their impressions. In the Relay Team, transitions must be carefully attended to.

Although the Relay Team is not easily used by a first-person narrator, I include it here as a strategy just to round out the possibilities. The challenge of the Relay Team approach is that of transition, as you move from one point of view to another. From sentence to sentence, paragraph to paragraph, the narrative must move smoothly, come to one person, release them, move on, fluidly linking and leaving.

The much-edited scene below is a catered wedding reception in the 1950s. The bride and groom, Matt March and Eden Douglass, eloped to Mexico, and are returning on this day to Matt's home for a reception. The two families have never met, and they are understandably wary of one another. Matt's family is comprised of only two elderly

Italians: his mother, Stella, and his uncle, Ernesto. Eden comes from a vast tribe of Mormons.

## WELCOME TO THE BRIDE AND GROOM

Like Stella, Ernesto was appalled as the Douglasses descended on their home, as car after car disgorged fussy children, screaming babies, uncomfortable matrons and men ill at ease in Sunday suits, all of them hot, weary from the long drive. Children, big and small, swooped down upon the once-quiet garden like Goths intent on sacking Rome . . .

Eden's relatives came to welcome the bride and groom, and stayed to pass judgment on the strange food, and the presence of alcohol. Of Eden's family only Tom Lance, Jr., and his French wife were drinking. They wore their mutual dissatisfaction visible as combat medals; like tired soldiers, they smoked without speaking. Their three bratty daughters, unsupervised, picked fights among themselves, and when that activity paled, they ganged up on the other kids, pelting them with the tomatoes from Ernesto's carefully tended plants The vegetable wars ended in tears and messed dresses, and one the Epps boys got pushed in the fountain, his wet backside swatted, right there on the spot by his mother . . .

Eden's cousin Bessie and her husband Nephi watched the antics of their own unruly children with the stolidity of mules linked to their traces. . . . Carrying heavy trays, waiters offered cold beers, wine and lemonade. Bessie and Nephi accepted only lemonade though Bessie's teenage son and his cousins, Micah and Jonah, managed to snag beers, and feel like men of the world, as long as they stayed out of Afton's sight.

Afton, flanked by Tom and Lil, clutched her lemonade in one hand, her hanky in the other. The sisters wore identical hats and gloves. . . . Tom wondered aloud what foreigners had against real food. Lil wondered aloud if Mexican marriages were even legal. Afton choked and sniffed back tears: "Eden has broken my heart.

I loved that girl like my own daughter. And now she's coming back from a Mexican marriage to a Catholic."

... Just then a cheer rose up! Mr. and Mrs. Matt March came through the gate and into the sunlit garden while the fountain splashed musically. . . . Eden was radiant with happiness. Matt, grinning, kept an arm around her waist, . . . though he clearly was surprised to see so many people.

Beaming, Matt made his way to Stella, took his mother in his arms while Stella stroked his face, and wept. "Mama," he said tenderly, "this is my wife, Eden."

Stella kissed Eden's cheeks, and said, "Oh my dear, you're so much better looking than his first wife."

"Oh Mama, no!" cried Matt.

"His what?" asked Eden.

"It's true," Stella sighed and nodded, "she is better looking."

## Enhancing the Crowd Scene

In creating your crowd scenes, pay particular attention to the nouns and verbs appropriate to the venue and the mood you want to convey. As with our earlier discussion of scenic depiction in "Lost Domains," bring in sensory information to underscore. What kind of people and where they are: Milling around a grungy bus station? A rock concert? A battlefield? Fourth of July at the beach? An airplane departure lounge? Or, as in Cheryl McCarthy's family memoir, *Many Hands Make Light Work*, nine kids renovating old Victorian houses together (nearly every scene in her memoir is a crowd scene!).

Specifics to consider for enhancing your crowd scene:

NOISE! Are these people shouting? In unison? Are they a choir? Or a protesting mob? Or are they huddled, conspiring in the library? Or whispering gossip over a tea table?

AMBIENT NOISE around the crowd: ear-splitting rock music spewing over a stadium? Honking horns? Parents shouting encouragement at a Little League game? A cacophony of cell phones?

CONSIDER THE SENSORY EFFECTS. Heat or cold or light or darkness. Is this crowd sweltering under a tropical sun while they wait in line for supplies after a hurricane? Are they numb with cold stuck on a broken-down bus on a mountain pass in winter?

CONSIDER MOOD AND UNDERCURRENTS. A backyard barbecue will be different than a memorial service. A holiday party at an elementary school will be different than the holiday party at the homeless shelter. Are your people in peril, or drugged or drunk or tense? Are they joyful, dispirited, or content?

PACE AND MOMENTUM. How will you pace your crowd scene? Does the action come to some kind of peak and then slowly diminish? This is how that first party scene at Gatsby's ends, Nick stumbling home in the dawn. Or does your scene end abruptly, as in the brief St. Elmo cop shop once Reverend Reedy's number is called? Or at the Elvis party with the arrival of the cops? Pace and momentum are questions best addressed in revision, once you have an overall sense of the action itself.

Have a writerly read of crowd scenes in books you admire. Ask yourself, what technique has the author used to move the reader through crowd? What nouns and verbs are at work here? What kind of pace and momentum inform the scene?

## Dialogue and the Crowd Scene

Crowd scenes create extra challenges for dialogue. Clearly, you don't want to waste a lot of narrative space or time assigning dialogue to characters who are (more or less) wallpaper: there for the effect, but not to be differentiated. Sometimes all you need of other people's dialogue is the suggestion of their words and voices, but done in such a way so as not to detract from your purpose. You can use italics to convey dialogue floating over the scene, coming from sources you do not want to identify singly, to suggest dialogue that requires no response, or dialogue that is created primarily for mood or ambience. In the Hamilton Reedy excerpt at the cop shop, there is no quoted dialogue at all until the duty officer calls out Hamilton's number, effectively breaking the spell. In the Elvis party scene, there are only two lines of dialogue, both conventionally offered (i.e., in quotes), but only one is emotionally significant; the other, Uncle Phil's, only serves to move the girls into the living room.

But what if your crowd scene is not a raucous police station, or a protest march, or a stadium for that matter? What if you need to use your crowd scene to convey pertinent information, and to suggest character? (As does Chapter 1 in the *Great Gatsby*, noted in the dialogue chapter.) Again, *The Great Gatsby* offers writers a fine how-to guide. Remember the other party early in the book, the rather squalid Do in Myrtle's apartment in New York? At Tom Buchanan's invitation, Nick goes into the city with him. Tom's mistress, Myrtle Wilson, joins them, and after they stop off at the bootlegger's, they all go to the apartment Tom rents for Myrtle where many people join them. Again, Nick is the Implicated Narrator, getting drunk with everyone else. But for narrative purposes this party requires far more than voices floating like amorphous banners. *In order to serve the narrative, Fitzgerald needs specific dialogue to convey information* to Nick (and thus, to the reader) about Myrtle, her hapless husband George, and her affair with Tom. So Myrtle's sister, Catherine, is present and chats up Nick at great length; among other things Catherine confides in Nick that Tom is Myrtle's first "sweetie," and Tom cannot divorce Daisy because she is a Catholic. (Nick knows Daisy is not Catholic.) Myrtle herself emerges from the bedroom and talks to Nick, telling how she met Tom, and a few pathetic anecdotes of her life with her husband, George. Present, too, are couple of colossal bores, neighbors in the building, Mr. McKee and his wife. Mr. McKee runs a photography studio, and at the end of the night Nick finds himself drearily going through photo albums of McKee's awful work before the last paragraph, where he blearily awaits the 4 a.m. train out of Penn Station.

At this sordid party, the dialogue *combines* with ambience to convey information we need to know about Myrtle's affair with Tom, but also to create the impression of narrow lives, maundering drunkenness, and moral squalor that erupts in domestic violence when Tom slaps Myrtle across the face, drawing blood, for her having uttered Daisy's sacred name.

What if your crowd scene is simpler, more along the lines of an ordinary dinner party? Once you have multiple speakers talking, it is all the more important that the dialogue is properly attributed, and that the speaker's actions and their words are all in the same paragraph. Also, your readers should be able to differentiate among their voices, their styles of expression, and the gestures affiliated with each. At an ordinary dinner party, much of the conversation may be typically banal. How can the writer achieve the effect of banal exchange without having to endure it? How much is too much?

The edited excerpt below is from a scene in my novel, *Three Strange Angels*. It takes place in 1950 in Hollywood at the palatial home of a studio executive, Roy Rosenbaum. The point of view is Quentin Castle, a young British literary agent, who, as representative of Castle Literary, has only just that afternoon arrived in Los Angeles. Quentin has been sent there to escort back to England the body of a renowned British novelist, Francis (Frank) Carson. Frank had been in Hollywood while Regent Pictures was filming his novel, *Some of These Days*, when he accidentally died by drowning. Though Quentin has come on behalf of the firm, he was not Frank's agent, and indeed he did not know Frank. Quentin is an Implicated Narrator as alcohol, disorientation, and jet lag undermine (or overwhelm) his senses. Note too which elements of conversation are given in actual quoted dialogue, and those that are elided over, merely alluded to.

## THE PERILS OF TRAVEL

A tall, casually dressed man with silver hair rose, took Quentin's hand, and introduced himself as Roy Rosenbaum. "My wife, Doris,"

he pointed to a woman who wore an expression of practiced seren-
ity. "My daughter, Lois, and her husband Aaron. We are so sorry
for your loss, Mr. Castle. We were all devastated. We are ready for
you. We have what you need," added Roy with a sad smile. "What
a talent Frank had. Never have I met anyone with such creative
flair. What are you drinking?"

"Gin and tonic," said Quentin, surprised to have an icy glass
instantly thrust into his hand. "Thank you."

"Was it a grueling journey? Did you fly?" asked Doris.

"I came on the Queen Mary to New York, and flew from there."

They all agreed that the big airplanes were bad for you, that
they took your body and put it down in one place when your mind
was still in another. The only truly refined travel was on the great
ocean liners. Doris went on at length about the Cunard liner they
had sailed on last spring when they went to England. She waxed
eloquent about the amenities until Roy coughed and put a fresh gin
and tonic in Quentin's hand. . . .

"As Frank's friend, you must be devastated by his death," said
Roy. "He was a remarkable talent. A great writer."

"Perhaps he was a great writer," said Lois with a sniff, "but he
could be very abrasive. At parties he propositioned all the women,
and if they didn't go to bed with him, he'd sing dirty songs, and
use their names in the lyrics. Really, Daddy, I don't know why you
tolerated him, all that bad behavior you wouldn't put up with from
anyone else."

Beneath his tan, Roy flushed slightly. "He wasn't like anyone
else."

"It's sad," Doris mused, "but perhaps his death will spark new
interest in his work."

"Undoubtedly," Quentin replied. "My father says Selwyn and
Archer will publish a new edition of *Some of These Days* within
a week." He sipped the unusually icy drink. "English literature lost
three great authors in as many weeks, Orwell, McVicar, and Carson."

"Did George Orwell die?" asked Aaron, rather stunned.

"January 21st," Quentin replied.

"I don't believe I know the name McVicar," said Roy.

Quentin described the great climber's exploits, books that had filled the British reading public with vicarious adventure. Roy and Aaron agreed such books were unsuited to pictures, too expensive to produce. Orwell's work was too gray and grim, but Francis Carson! All those headlong love affairs! All that opulent romance! Their talk then turned to a string of American pictures, American names, discussed in a jargon that reminded Quentin of a conversation he had once tried to have with a Scotsman while on a walking tour in the Hebrides where they both spoke English, but neither could understand the other.

"I'm afraid we're boring Quentin," said Roy.

"Not at all."

"When do you leave?" asked Aaron.

"Tuesday I fly to New York. I'm booked for the Queen Mary next Wednesday, the weekly return to England."

They all agreed once again that the great ocean liners were a far more civilized way to travel than the airplane. Doris reiterated how pleasant was their last sailing to England, their first trip since the War, though sadly, they had found England. . . . She sought some elusive description.

"Austere," said Quentin. "We live in an age of austerity." The very word seemed to waft over them like the pale smoke from their cigarettes. Quentin added that though the British had won the war—he included their American allies, naturally—in England, memory lingered amid the ruins and losses. His having evoked this unhappy past lay uneasily upon people whose faces were resolutely towards the sunlit future.

The white-jacketed black man arrived and announced dinner was ready. Doris rose in a rustle of chiffon and took Quentin's arm. She led him to the dining room, chatting all the while about Harrods, and the hotels and the country houses where they had stayed last spring, the titled people they had met, none of whom Quentin knew, not even the names.

Fatigue, disorientation, two drinks on an empty stomach, his wine glass constantly refilled. Everyone except Roy drank lavishly, and empty bottles vanished at the hands of nearly invisible servants, and new ones took their place. The unfamiliar food, unfamiliar voices, unfamiliar topics of conversation all heightened Quentin's sense of being somehow tested and found wanting. His understanding rose and ebbed. He chewed reflectively on what seemed to him nearly raw meat, thinking of T. S. Eliot and do I dare to eat a peach. . . . When conversation lulled he said, apropos of nothing, "I must say, it seems very odd to me that Francis Carson would drown in a swimming pool. They say he was a strong swimmer. He used to live on the Sussex coast and swim in the English Channel." Did he imagine that they all paused, forks midway to their lips?

"The coroner's report came in. We have it for you," said Aaron. "Accidental death by drowning. He was very drunk when he fell in the pool."

Lois said, "Everyone treated Frank well, and that's how he repays us?"

"Are you referring to his dying?" asked Quentin. Clearly, he was failing to grasp some essential underthread, not simply what was being said, but what was being implied. He gulped from his water glass, thus far untouched.

"Francis Carson was a great loss to everyone artistically, but a great personal loss to all of us," said Roy, sounding like a parson delivering a sermon to known sinners. . . ."He was at the prime of his artistic life, and his death will be long felt. We loved his book, and he loved our movie."

"That's true," said Aaron.

"But I keep wondering," Quentin went on, "I mean, why did Francis Carson go into the pool? Did he just jump in? Did he fall in?"

"It was an accidental death," Roy reminded them.

"He was alone," said Aaron, "so no one knows the answer to your question, Quentin. There weren't any witnesses."

Roy made a gesture with his hand, and from a doorway, hitherto unseen persons emerged, cleared the plates, and laid clean forks for dessert, almond cheesecake which everyone assured Quentin he would love. . . .

"His death has upset everything," said Doris, her voice moist. "It's all so unseemly, and everyone here was so distraught, so unnerved, they had to shut down production."

"Yes," Aaron snapped, "and now we've got a lot people standing around collecting paychecks for doing nothing."

"Why can't you just give people a chance to grieve?" asked Doris.

"We did, dear," said Roy. "Now it's time to go back to work. Tomorrow, right Aaron? Cameras roll again tomorrow." He dabbed his lips with his napkin. "Everybody back on their heads." Roy laughed heartily; Aaron chortled, and the two women giggled irrepressibly.

All tension suddenly evaporated, but Quentin, bewildered, couldn't see anything funny.

## Prompt: Enhancing Your Memoir

Select a crowd scene (any situation with three or more people), and revise it in layers. Ask yourself if the Implicated Narrator or the Onlooker will best serve your story; that is, someone who partakes of the mood or action, or someone who stands apart and can be judgmental, or ironic. (The View From is a possibility depending on where you place your narrator.) Then quickly splash/dash/add sensory input and/or ambience, and revise for that. Finally, go back and season with dialogue as needed, whether you quote it, assign it, or italicize it, and let it simply float above the fray.

———

Crowd scenes can often serve as useful openers, as a sort of prologue to the memoir. For instance, remember Netta Gibbs's snapshot of the family in the backyard standing near the car that was to take Joe and the parents to the courthouse. If Netta took that info and made it scenic, it could function as a prologue of sorts, to root the central drama that will inform her childhood memoir. She could give each of the people in the photograph description and dialogue that would highlight who they are, what they are feeling. She could indicate the inward anxieties of everyone present (except maybe Joe; he was inscrutable). With this scene as prologue, the reader could have a swift introduction to the whole family, all gathered in one place.

This is basically the function that the opening scene of Francis Ford Coppola's *The Godfather*, the film, explores. (The book opens differently.) That wedding scene, look at it carefully and you will see that every character, major and minor, has just enough screen time, just enough dialogue—sometimes no more than a single line and a few seconds—that serves to indicate who they are, their faults, their flaws, and, in some cases, their fates. This scene uses the Relay Team. Against a panoply of color and activity and music, as the camera moves among the crowd, you see avarice, anger, lust, social discomfort, stolid loyalty. You see the functioning of tradition, the parsing of favors, the code of justice Don Corleone subscribes to. You see the plight of the pregnant wife and her unfaithful husband, the giggling, eager girlfriend, the careless bride. You see Michael tell his naïve WASP girlfriend he's not like the rest of them. And then, with all that accomplished, and though the party is clearly going to go on for a long time, the scene is over. You, the viewer, have all you need, a veritable index of characters.

F. Scott Fitzgerald and Charles Dickens are the maestros of the crowd scene. Both authors clearly relished the energies implicit in social settings and reveled in the ways in which interactions expose character. Moreover, they knew how to infuse their crowd scenes with emotions. The lovely opening beach scene in *Tender Is the Night* and the party that follows resonate throughout the novel. Dick Diver, the central character, says ironically, "I want to give a really bad party ..." and he will get his wish, though not in the way he meant. That party will delineate the major characters, even though the scene itself is told from the point of view of Rosemary Hoyt, who is an Onlooker, an outsider who does not know anyone well, moreover an actress who has a camera call in the morning and cannot drink as much as the others.

Charles Dickens is the consummate writer not merely of crowds, but of mobs, and all that throbs beneath the mob's chaotic actions. Chapter 5 in A *Tale of Two Cities* where the wine cask breaks open in the rue St. Antoine (quoted very briefly at the beginning of this chapter) and the threadbare, impoverished Parisians fall to their knees in the street, bend over, and slurp it up from the cobblestones; really, that's all you need to know about the causes of the French Revolution, never mind the oceans of ink spilled on the subject since 1789.

# 9 | Researching the Memoir

*When from a long distant past nothing subsists, after the people
are dead, after the things are broken and scattered, taste and smell
alone, more fragile but more enduring, more unsubstantial, more
persistent, more faithful, remains poised for a long time, like souls
remembering, waiting, hoping amid the ruins of all the rest; and bear
unflinchingly, in the tiny and almost impalpable drop of their essence,
the vast structure of recollection.*
—Marcel Proust, *Remembrance of Things Past*

I have a particular fondness for the whir of the old microfilm machines. A special affection for the clunky thunking of the reels
as you pop them on the spindles and once they're on, and you've
threaded the film through to the other side, inevitably it's upside
down and you have to turn the whole plate around to be able to read.
That done, you spin the handle on the right while the black-and-white
text races past your eyes in a blur of gray. For the historical novels
I've written, the last stop in the late drafts are long afternoons in the
library with microfilm readers and a legal pad for taking notes. For the
novel *Caveat* (quoted in chapter 5), before I put together the last drafts
I went to the library, and amid the boxes of microfilm for the *New
York Times*, I selected November 1916. I put that reel on the reader
and spun through the pages. Although the conversation between Dr.
Tipton and Hank Beecham did not actually describe what was in
those headlines, at least I, the author, knew what was happening on
the Western Front. For *Three Strange Angels* (quoted in chapter 8),
I went to the London *Times* in January 1950 when the novel begins,
and I began whirring through that historical moment. I was able to
invoke in my book the weather, the dreary headlines, rationing, and
the like. The past to me was the present to them.

I have passed happy hours in front of these microfilm machines, but when I finally stumble out of the library I always feel a little hungover, like the kid at the end of *Where the Wild Things Are*. Certainly that's how I felt some years ago after whirring through microfilm copies of the *Sun-Telegram* in the San Bernardino public library. I was looking for articles written by Winifred Martin, who had been the paper's "society editor." Until perhaps the 1970s, local newspapers' "society pages" served as a sort of Facebook, chronicling weddings and engagements and travel plans, graduations and charity events, choir practices, talent contests, beauty contests, science fairs and Eagle Scout ceremonies, the Masons, the Elks, and various other accounts of "fine jollifications." Miss Martin served as the paper's "society editor" for nearly forty years, literally until the day she died in about 1961. After her death, the *Sun-Telegram* (then family-owned) set up, in her honor, the Winifred Martin Prize for the Best Girl Journalist in San Bernardino. The year I graduated from high school, I won this award. (There were only two high schools in the city, so it wasn't exactly competing for the Best Girl Journalist Pulitzer.) It came with a pen set and one hundred dollars. That was my only connection with Winifred Martin. And yet . . . for reasons I still cannot quite fathom, years later, in the mid-1990s Winifred Martin started to haunt me. So much so that on one of our family jaunts to Southern California, I went to the public library and, beginning in the 1930s (that would have been her heyday), I sought out her daily columns.

Microfilm, of course, has no indexes, and indeed, no way whatsoever to cue a certain name or even the name of a recurring column or any such thing, so, willy-nilly, I spun through the material like a roulette wheel. This utterly random process was certainly not efficient. Without any sort of "bead" on where to stop, I stumbled on all sorts of surprises quite apart from Miss Martin. Look! Here is a photo of Miss D, a high school administrator I knew as a withered, joyless prune, but here she is, Miss D, smiling and vibrant, quite lovely, at some local soiree. Here's Mr. R, that grim curmudgeon of a math teacher, beaming in his wedding picture! Names, even without photos, leaped up and off the gray film; parents, grandparents, relatives of high school classmates I had long forgotten. Moving forward in time to the era in which I was growing up, and the *Sun-Telegram* came daily to our house, I was astonished to come upon a photo of half a dozen businessmen, pillars-of-the-community types who stood flanking a lovely teenage girl who had just been crowned Miss Whatever of 1961. I was horrified to see their grins! These middle-aged dudes are so clearly leching all over this girl! Enough to make your skin crawl! One of these men was a neighbor. Except for the microfilm machine, I would never have thought that the neighbor could look so freaking creepy, or that Miss D had once been a cheerful belle, or that Mr. R had once been a happy man.

You, dear writer, can be spared the microfilm machine if you want, and the drafty basement of the city library. You can have the pleasures of discovering newspapers to enrich your memoir for a reasonable fee. A subscription service will put thousands of newspapers at your fingertips, and they will also index for you and seek out key names, and you can do this work in your jammies. What you discover will come at you afresh, and with an emotional punch (like the lecherous-looking neighbor). The ads, the fashions, the high school sports, the tax levies, fires, crimes, elections, businesses opening or closing, all whirl to offer you instant, refreshed context for your memoir. Especially in the "society pages," the further back in time you go, the more numerous and detailed are these stories, often told in a chirpy, chatty fashion, rippling with the sort of detail that writers treasure—who wore what, who was present, where did the bride live, and so on. Oftentimes you can put this kind of info together with what you know, or what has been told to you, along with family photos, and bring your memoir into much sharper scenic focus.

Especially if you can access a hometown paper, go look at the date on which you were born. What kind of world were you born into? Your mama and daddy might have had eyes only for you, but the rest of the world went on, moved forward unaware that you had joined humanity. Look up any other day or season important to your memoir and see the events that swirled and shaped the world in which your personal life unfolded. This is not to say that these major events should necessarily impinge on your narrative, but the effort will certainly broaden your perspective.

Indeed, researching your memoir can bring you into possession of material that you had no idea even existed. Peggy Kalpakian Johnson intended to include in her *Centennial Memoir* a chapter about Miss Grace Towner, the American Congregationalist missionary teacher in the Adana Girls Seminary where my Armenian grandmother, Haigouhi, was a day student. The Armenians were, for centuries, an ethnic minority in Turkey, and in 1915, under cover of war, the Ottomans began the systematic purge of the Armenian population, resulting in 1 to 1.5 million deaths. (Thus the term "the starving Armenians," which raises the hackles and pierces the heart no matter that a hundred years have passed.) Adana was a major city in southeastern Turkey. As an American missionary, Miss Towner would have had broad contacts with the many other missionaries all over Turkey, and thus be aware that what was happening to Armenians elsewhere was about to happen to Armenians in Adana. She came to Haigouhi's home and asked her mother if Haigouhi could become a boarding student at the school. To earn her keep, Haigouhi could do chores. Her mother agreed. Haigouhi, age fourteen, never saw her mother again. Haigouhi's mother and father and little brother were marched into the desert to die, but Haigouhi was safe in the Adana Girls Seminary, where Miss Towner instructed the girls to lay an American flag on the flat roof so that any combatants flying overhead would know this was American property. (America did not enter the war until April of 1917.) Many years later, in 1953, through an incredible intersection of fate and circumstance, Miss Towner (now living in a missionary retirement home near Los Angeles) was reunited with my grandmother and her family. As a small child I even met her. We all owed our lives to her bravery.

Peggy Kalpakian Johnson wrote up the story of this incredible 1953 reunion for a memoir anthology called *So Much Depends.* The reunion itself was the point of the story, which was short, seven hundred words. However, the editor informed Peggy that each essay needed to be twelve hundred words. Peggy had already written all she knew of the Miss Towner story (all any of us knew), so she took steps to find out more.

At age ninety-five Peggy Johnson Googled Grace Towner (1883–1968). She found out Grace was from Osborne, Kansas. I wrote to the Osborne Historical Society, who sent a packet of materials (and I sent a donation). We discovered that Grace had graduated from Washburn College in Topeka, Kansas, in 1909, and online we "met" the Washburn reference librarian. Reference librarians are generally eager to respond to inquiries and to direct writers to sources that can help answer their questions. This Washburn University librarian was wonderfully helpful, and she seemed to enjoy the discoveries as much as we did. She sent me many links and info. I followed them down all sorts of rabbit holes, spent long hours reading the online archives of the Osborne *Farmer* newspaper, an absolute trove of info. From that newspaper I learned when Grace went to visit her sister who was having a baby, and that her sister had died in childbirth, that Grace once fell off a horse and broke her arm, and the topic of her high school graduation speech in 1902, one of a class of four. This librarian directed me to the online archives of the missionary association in which Grace served, further deepening and broadening our understanding. Through this librarian's generous guidance, we learned so much, and Peggy was better able to portray a courageous woman whose life and deeds have otherwise vanished.

The Internet may be a viper's nest, but for researchers and writers, it is a godsend. Many ethnic and cultural groups have their own archives, sometimes, but not always, housed in university libraries. Local historical societies may not have records online, but in my experience their staffs, even tiny staffs of volunteers, are always helpful. Churches and missionary societies all have documentary records, some in scrawled handwritten notes, of their work records, who traveled where, how long they stayed there, and occasionally their obituaries. This information was especially helpful in researching Miss Towner and the women missionaries and teachers with whom she worked in Turkey.

In addition to university and public-library reference librarians, historical societies, and newspapers, there are services that, for a fee, can connect you with high school yearbooks from just about anywhere over decades. High school yearbooks reek of the *Now*, of what was important to the kids who lived it, however silly that *Now* may appear in retrospect. Parsing through these pages will, trust me, bring it all back vividly. Many public records, including census records and property tax records as well as lawsuits, are available online. One of the pleasures of Sarah Broom's prize-winning memoir, *The Yellow House*, is watching how skillfully the author, late in the book, uses public land-use records and permits to document the decay of her Eastern New Orleans neighborhood. Researching these records enriched her book, but Broom did not do this online. She actually sat in drafty waiting rooms and dealt with uncongenial clerks, and she got her fingers dirty with the dust and ink of old files.

Ellis Island has archives essential for anyone writing a memoir of an immigrant family. (You can find out what they brought with them, down to the needles and thread, how much money they had in hand, and who were their traveling companions!) The Church of Jesus Christ of Latter-day Saints maintains acres of important genealogical records and a fine, knowledgeable staff who are willing to help direct inquiries. Any of these sorts of sources can deepen, broaden, and enliven your understanding of the past and the people in your past.

## The Vapor Trail

But there are other avenues to research your memoir—not high school pictures or citizenship papers, not deeds or lawsuits or divorce decrees, nothing so telling as those paper trails. I think of it as a vapor trail sidestepping the usual cues and moving through an associational ether where memory is instantly, if ephemerally, enhanced.

## MUSIC

Music bypasses all those synaptic gray cells needed to do trigonometry, or to recite Robert Frost's poetry, or to remember where you put the dog's leash. In the words of one of my musician friends, "Music moves where words can't never go. Words are a linear process. Music's a feeling. Words have to go through your head. Music comes up from your heart, your guts, your groin." Music can quell or unleash passions, can go to places long shuttered, can make the heart soar, can bring people to long-suppressed tears.

For Christmas 1989, we gave my dad a trumpet, an instrument he had played as a boy. He was delighted with the gift, and though he didn't play it very much, he started to talk about the music and what it had meant to him. How Bill Johnson came by his first trumpet, a cornet, is a story in itself, though not for here. Suffice it to say, as the eldest son of an impoverished family, he never had a lesson. In 1935, at a statewide competition in Pocatello, Bill Johnson was judged to be the best high school trumpet player in the whole state of Idaho, probably one of the happiest moments of his whole ninety-four years. The piece he won with was "Bride of the Waves," written by Herbert L. Clarke, famous in its day (1904) and a standard still in the 1930s.

Some years later I found a CD of Herbert L. Clarke's (1867–1945) original recordings. I thought I would surprise my dad with this wonderful find. My parents came to my house, and I said to my dad, "Sit down. I have a surprise for you!" I set the CD play to track 4, "Bride of the Waves." The expressions that flitted swiftly across my father's face are beyond my powers of description, and then he put his face in his hands and began to sob. I had never seen him cry. Maybe my mother had seen him cry when his father died, or when my sister was desperately ill, or when my brother was in Vietnam, but me, no. I had never seen him cry.

Clearly, to bypass cerebral synapses to elicit emotion instantly, music needn't be brilliant, not Beethoven's *Fifth Symphony*, or Ravel's *Bolero*, or Joni Mitchell, or Paul Simon for that matter. Admit it, dear writer, there are commercial jingles from when you were eight years old that you can still sing. There are theme songs from long-ago (and best-forgotten) television sitcoms that if you were declared brain-dead, laid out there, sheeted on the table, and someone played that theme into your ear, you'd wake up and identify the source.

Using popular music can enhance your memoir by bypassing memory. In perhaps the last twenty-five years American popular music has shattered into niches. (The standard joke is now there is no Top 40, only the Top 43,000.) But American popular music was once generally allied not simply with era, but with season. Back when radio, even AM radio, was the only means of entertainment in your car, or in your kitchen, or in your garage, DJs played certain songs that changed week by week, month by month, era by era. Finding this music, playing it, will take you straying off the tidy trail you have carved through the thicket of the past and lead you, perhaps viscerally, to some more vivid truth or moment. Moreover, if you are of the LP era (when one song on the album followed another in a carefully curated order), in your head you'll hear the song following before the first one even ends.

Netta Gibbs wrote that while she and Granny were belting out "Amazing Grace," the rest of the world was listening to "Dancing Queen." How might it serve her memoir to revise to the music of the "Dancing Queen" vintage alongside the hymns she sang in church when, with her bright young voice, she was thought to be a holy prodigy. Think about what was playing on the radio during the road trips of your youth, or family vacations, or the year you graduated from high school, or got drafted, or suffered a traumatic illness. Perhaps the summer of saccharine, excruciatingly stupid love songs, "Build Me Up, Buttercup," "Crimson and Clover," "Sugar, Sugar, Honey, Honey," is the era in which those silly songs somehow brought comfort, or made you cry, or made you laugh, and for that reason these bubble-gum songs remain more indelible than the profound "Sounds of Silence." Maybe Pink Floyd's "Comfortably Numb" was an unlooked-for anthem for an era in your life. Or Queen and David

Bowie's "Under Pressure" all too well described one particular season. Perhaps Tina Turner's "What's Love Got to Do With It?" reverberates over a love affair, or a divorce, or a prom night. Perhaps the soundtrack from the Mario Brothers video game takes you right back to playing video games in the basement of your parents' house. The question here is not: Are these great songs, or great artists? The question is: What do they trigger in your heart and mind and memory? If you're brave enough to sidestep those manicured paths of memory, find the music and have at it, inhabit the thrumming nexus where the events of your life intersected with this music.

PROMPT: MUSIC AND THE MEMOIR   Find your era. Seek out the songs, make a loose playlist, organize it on your favorite medium. (I am sidestepping altogether *how* you might access the music because any advice I have will be passé-unto-laughable by next month.) Save the current version of your draft. Put on your headphones or earbuds, or simply turn up the volume and play that music while you revise, say, Chapter 2 with Music, not just once, but again and again. Let that music throb, or lilt, or waft beyond the brain, like aural lightning illuminating otherwise dark landscapes.

HISTORICALLY AMBIENT MUSIC   The era of recorded music began in about 1888. At that time a wealthy American, enamored of the newfangled Edison cylinders, took them with him to London and recorded the voices of famous guests at fashionable London dinner parties. One of these was Sir Arthur Sullivan of Gilbert and Sullivan fame. On October 5, 1888, here are the words the composer spoke into the cylinder: "Dear Mr. Edison, for myself I can only say that I am astonished and somewhat horrified at the results of this evening's experiment. Astonished at the wonderful [?] you have developed and terrified at the thought that so much [?] and bad music may be put on record forever. But all the same, I think it is the most wonderful thing that I have ever experienced, and I congratulate you with all my heart on this wonderful discovery."

I've always thought this an odd comment for a composer. One would have thought Arthur Sullivan would have been unabashedly delighted that musical performances—hitherto lost to the upper reaches of the theatre and the passing moment—could be preserved. (Perhaps he anticipated "Sugar, Sugar, Honey, Honey.") Nonetheless much of this early recorded, vintage music has been made available to the general public online, through various collections, including the Smithsonian Institute. (Any of these online caches will fill fascinating hours spent listening.)

Thus, if you are writing a memoir that reaches back into history, into eras you have to reconstruct, it's easily possible to have access to the music that permeated that era, even before the radio. You can listen to early recordings of the stirring songs of the Great War, speeches and music from the Suffragist era, Broadway melodies, including timeless classics from George Gershwin and Jerome Kern, as well as bright, popular ditties like "Barney Google and his Goo-Goo-Googly Eyes." The great Alan Lomax catalog of prison songs and field songs and hymns is available, rough and grainy and soul-searing to this day. Selecting through these possibilities, creating a playlist, and then playing this music *while you revise* can brighten and heighten your portrayal of your people, their circumstances, and their era.

EMOTIONALLY AMBIENT MUSIC  Emotionally ambient music is not historical, and it will not appear on the page. Emotionally ambient music is a writing tool that can affect (and have an effect upon) the mood or tenor of the scene under construction. Its function is to free up your imagination, unhook your mental dependence on cause-effect-if-this-then-that. Emotionally ambient music is particularly useful for scenes that are freighted with feeling, ambivalence, drama. In my novel *American Cookery*, to portray the suicide of an important character, I turned to the music of Ennio Morricone, more particularly to the album of Yo Yo Ma playing a selection of Ennio Morricone's work. The scene was short and wrenching; I rewrote it many times over, often in tears as I played this album. In these rewritings, I gave myself free reign for error. Overdoing it? Fine. Too much? Fine. Basically repetitive? Fine. As I wrote and rewrote and while the music washed over me, the scene finally resolved itself into something spare, relying on carefully curated sounds and visuals. For the final few revisions I did not listen to Yo Yo Ma. What I had needed from him and the maestro, Morricone, was already in the prose, though not, technically, on the page. I occasionally make playlists allied to certain characters, or certain sequences even if they're not fraught, as in the depiction of the suicide. These playlists function as homemade soundtracks for scenes. I play them on repeat while I'm writing for several drafts before I turn them off. By then the homemade soundtrack is situated in my head.

Indeed, film soundtracks are a good place to seek out emotionally ambient music in general. *Zorba the Greek*, a British film released in 1966, is not at all allied to my mother's *Centennial Memoir*, but she listened to the soundtrack (by Mikis Theodorkaris) while she wrote certain passages. There are chants on the *Zorba* soundtrack that remind her of her father singing in the morning while he shaved; music was very important to him.

On any given soundtrack, each piece will have some thematic core. Themes are often allied to certain characters, or incidents, and so recur in slightly different forms throughout the album. The most vivid statement of these themes will probably be in the opening credits and closing credits. The ease of streaming means you can pick and choose, pluck out those that interrupt the mood you are trying to create, and go with those that suit the mood you are trying to elicit.

Here are some search suggestions, cues, as it were, for soundtrack composers.

- Elmer Bernstein (d. August 2004), Jerry Goldsmith (d. July 2004), and Ennio Morricone (d. 2020) have a vast range of possibility if only for the sheer length and breadth of their careers over decades. (All three often composed music that was sometimes far better than the films it was written for.)

Somewhere in their work you can probably find almost any kind of emotionally ambient music.

- For an easygoing vibe, see the work of Randy Newman (*Toy Story*).
- For sheer terror, see Bernard Herrmann (d. 1975), who wrote Hitchcock scores, *Citizen Kane*, and *Taxi Driver*.
- For jazzy breadth and brassy brilliance, see Nino Rota (d. 1979), *The Godfather*, and nearly all the Fellini films, including the haunting theme to *La Strada*.
- For orchestral pomp, see Howard Shore's scores to the *Lord of the Rings* trilogy; for a Celtic touch his score for *The Departed*.
- Danny Elfman's scores (*Nightmare Before Christmas*, *Edward Scissorhands*) zap between the haunting and the manic; they have an electric, nervous, jumpy quality.
- James Horner (d. 2015) is best known for his vast, romantic scores to *Titanic* and *Braveheart*.
- T. Bone Burnett has put together Americana source-music soundtracks (*O Brother Where Art Thou*, *Cold Mountain*).
- Terence Blanchard is known for his contribution to jazz, but his film work includes the HBO documentary *When the Levees Broke*, about Hurricane Katrina, and *BlacKkKlansman*.
- Maurice Jarre's (d. 2009) soundtracks often have a martial element. He is famous for his work on David Lean epics, *Lawrence in Arabia* and *Dr. Zhivago*.
- Hans Zimmer's scores are eclectic, expansive, and across a broad swath of genre, including the various *Pirates of the Caribbean* films.
- Others contemporary screen composers include Eric Serra, Gabriel Yared, Patrick Doyle, Rachel Portman, Bruce Broughton, James Newton Howard, Thomas Newman, and of course, Bear McCreary.

Emotionally ambient music is usually most effective without lyrics. You don't need to know the verses of "Danny Boy" to get misty on hearing those opening strains, ditto (at least for me) for "Over the Sea to Skye," "Kathleen Mavourneen," and "Sometimes I Feel Like a Motherless Child," or "Summertime." The power of a song to retain its emotional strength across generations (never mind the lyrics) can be heard, for instance, on Ken Burns's *The Civil War* soundtrack. He uses two versions of "Marching Through Georgia": one crisp, bright, jaunty, up-tempo, as it might have been played by Union bands and heard by Union troops; the other slow, dirgelike, haunting, heart-breaking as it would have been heard by those whose homes and lands were being marched through.

Even the most hackneyed tunes can carry emotional weight. Hymns, for instance. Even if you're not of a religious cast of mind or background, there's often something about these old war-horse hymns that can touch a resonant chord. I think particularly of two albums: "Come Sunday" and "Steal Away," by the jazz musicians Charlie Hayden and Hank Jones, with Hayden on bass and Jones on piano. Their rendering of these hymns and spirituals could reduce Attila the Hun to blubbering pulp. Ditto for the melodies of Thomas Moore (1779–1852) whose name might not be instantly familiar, but you might well recognize "The Minstrel Boy" and "The Last Rose of Summer," among others. Because these tunes are so old, they often come with a stuffy, saccharine, antiquated patina—which, after all, is what makes them hackneyed. You can find these songs (as with Herbert L. Clarke) in original or antique recordings, but also in albums of contemporary musicians who have fashioned this material into fresh, new arrangements.

Instrumental classical music can provide a rich source of emotionally ambience to help you write. Think, for instance, of Vivaldi's "The Four Seasons." Each of those has its own mood or tenor; anything you would write under the influence, say, of "Spring" would probably not come out the same if you wrote it while you listened to "Winter."

Below is an array of classical possibilities by mood—a strictly subjective list, and mostly French because they are my favorites.

- Pomp and opulence—the nineteenth century, Offenbach, Rossini, Viennese waltzes.
- Fragile, restrained—Erik Satie
- Moody, restless—Debussy, Ravel, Faure
- Unrestrained, unremitting energy—Beethoven, Liszt
- Elegance, energy—Mozart
- Wit and unlooked-for rhythms—Stravinsky and his lesser-known contemporaries, Auric and Antheil
- For both pomp and heartbreak, I think of Verdi and Puccini. I include opera in here because the lyrics are in Italian, and so the emotional resonance reaches the listener without benefit of knowing what they are actually saying.
- For a rich American orchestral sound, you have the classical work of Copland, Gershwin, and the lesser-known nineteenth-century New Orleans composer Louis Moreau Gottschalk (1820-1869) in whose work you can hear elements of ragtime and jazz, decades before they emerged into general popularity.

The uses of music in memoir are many and glorious. Be forewarned, though, once you have allied these songs or pieces to your memoir, they will stay there. After I wrote that *American Cookery* death scene to Yo Yo Ma and Ennio Morricone, I could never again listen to that album. If perchance, a track from that album comes on randomly, I experience an instant stab of loss in my heart, and I quickly turn to the next piece. If, dear writer, you have put in the time, effort, and emotional energy into layering your scene with "Sugar, Sugar, Honey, Honey," whenever you hear it, you will be instantly reminded of your writing moment, and not its original historical association in your life. Maybe that's a mercy.

There are other kinds of research that cannot actually be "done," but that exist as experiential moments to be harnessed in service of the memoir. Along with music, scent is, for me, a most powerful connector to the past. But scent, unlike music, cannot be found online.

However, it can be predicted. You know that every spring lilacs will bloom and that this particular scent will inevitably carry you back to . . . wherever you spent a certain spring. (The pain or glory of that moment might diminish after years. Or it might not.) The smell of a Christmas tree, that's indelible, not perhaps for a single Christmas, but for the cyclical revisiting of Christmas. The scent of cheap suntan lotion, or chlorine in a swimming pool, barbeque smoke, or night-blooming jasmine is redolent of summer. When you wander into these seasonal moments, give yourself leave to succumb to them. Make notes. Remember.

But there are other scents that cannot be relied upon, that can just happen to you, unbidden, unlooked-for, possibly even unwelcome. A certain fragrance, cologne, allied with a certain person from your past can knock you right back to childhood. Where are the blue vials of Evening in Paris that used to dot the vanity of my youngest aunt? Or my dad's Old Spice, or my sister's best friend who draped herself in Tabu? On a bus I once sat next to a woman wearing Estee Lauder cologne, and I wanted to put my arms around her, so powerfully did she evoke a dear friend I had not seen in years. Less pleasantly, Pine-Sol always takes me back to the girls' bathroom at Shirley Avenue Elementary School, which is why I do not use it.

When my eldest son was just a toddler, and we were living in Florida, I was making peach Jell-O for him. (Yes, my kids were definitely *not* the ones with the carrot-stick snacks.) I tore open the package, dumped it in the bowl, poured in the hot water, and suddenly fuming up, circling, swirling, out of that bowl, was not a sugary creation from Kraft Foods, but the smack-your-face re-creation of a certain summer *our peach tree dripped with peaches and my mother was determined to preserve them in the old fashioned way, laying out long sheets of cheesecloth across the picnic table in the hot California sun, and she and we were pitting those peaches as fast as we could, the juice covering our hands and dripping on to the cement driveway, and laying the peach halves on the cheesecloth and covering them with another layer of cheesecloth, and then, while she went on to some other task, I remained there for hours haplessly waving a flyswatter.*

This is not a memory of any great beauty or significance. But the recollection came to me, came at me, really, in an unlooked-for moment like a slap, and with such force and veracity, such intensity, that tears, unbidden, streamed down my face. I immediately stopped what I was doing and telephoned my mother in California, long-distance or not, and never mind she was at work at the hospital where she was secretary to an orthopedic surgeon. My mother reminded me that, ironically, what I remembered wasn't peaches at all, but apricots. We had a bumper crop of apricots that summer, and yes, she had tried to dry them in the sun, and it was a disaster; the whole went into the trash. But so what? The ephemeral enchantment, the power of the scent, that was authentic.

———

Research for the memoir is not at all plowing through tomes and marking passages with Post-it Notes. Research for the memoir is the art of seeking out, or stumbling upon, or rounding a corner in time past, recognizing that moment . . . and adding its richness to your work.

# 10 | Narrative Voice

*It's all in the art. You get no credit for living.*
—V. S. Pritchett (1900–1997), *The Cab at the Door* (1968)

Consider Ansel Adams's photographs of Half Dome at Yosemite. We marvel at the strength and beauty of these images, but no one would ever mistake the photograph for actually standing in the shadow of Half Dome. Thus it is with the memoir: the experience you convey on the page is not the living-through of those events, but their artful representation. Just as Ansel Adams had to set up his equipment and reflect on his timing before making his photographs, the author of the memoir must create the narrator, the literary construct used to tell the tale. The narrator is different from the author. When readers pick up a memoir—before they read a single word—what do they know about the author? That the author lived to tell the tale. What do they know about the narrator? That the tale needed to be told.

The author creates a narrator in order to serve the story. The author knows more than the narrator. The author does the winnowing (what to include, what to exclude), but the narrator is the voice that tells the tale. The narrative voice strikes a kind of intimacy. The tale itself will be influenced by the teller.

The memoir will always have a first-person narrator, but there are many sorts of narrative voices that create different effects. The narrative voice can be innocent or jaunty or elegiac, wry, tender, assessive, harsh, poetic, matter-of-fact; it can be colloquial or formal. The narrative voice in Henry Adams's classic, *The Education of Henry Adams* is so formal as to be almost opaque. The narrative voice in Rick Bragg's *All Over But the Shoutin'* is so easygoing, so full of casual grammar, that it creates the impression that you, the reader, are sitting at the bar with him having a beer, maybe more than one. (So powerful is Bragg's narrative voice, I once told a friend I had got it on audio, but I misremembered. I had read the book.) Mary Karr's *The Liar's Club* is told in a narrative voice so raucous, so boisterous, so energetic, it ricochets all over the place. The reader comes away from her every chapter more or less breathless. Patti Smith's *Just Kids* begins with the elegiac rendering of her hearing of the death of her longtime friend and former lover, Robert Mapplethorpe. But once her story moves back to the days of their shared youth in New York City, the narrative voice becomes jaunty, as if picking up the urban rhythms of the streets. Margo Jefferson's unique *Negroland* examines her past in terms of the influences (books, magazines, music, movies, the values of her well-to-do parents) that shaped her consciousness as a Black woman. Throughout, the narrative voice is crisp, terse, sometimes downright schoolmarmish.

Benjamin Franklin's *Autobiography* is misnamed; actually it's three memoir essays masquerading as a series of letters to his son. I say masquerading because clearly these memoirs are written for an unknown reader. In the first, Franklin (1706–1790) describes his hardscrabble youth, fleeing his punitive brother in Boston to arrive in Philadelphia, as a sort of wayward apprentice up for adventure. The tone here is lively, confident, gently self-effacing, and engaging. But the latter two chapters/essays are not about adventures. The narrator is now an established, prominent figure in Philadelphia, and moreover a citizen of the world. Franklin's experiences as a wise citizen are less compelling, certainly less winsome than his adventures as a young man. Now he is more interested in educating readers to become good citizens (like himself, naturally), and though the narrative voice remains informal by eighteenth-century standards, it is instructional. (The *New York Times* book critic Parul Sehgal describes his tone as "purring complacency.") Booker T. Washington's *Up From Slavery* follows the same pattern in both voice and content. The early chapters of *Up From Slavery* make for riveting reading, his childhood steeped in slavery, his youth seeking an education in Reconstruction South are dramatic, memorable. (You will never forget the anecdote of his mother stealing a cooked chicken from the big house one night, bringing it to her children, and waking them to eat it on the spot.) Booker T. Washington's (1856–1915) latter chapters, however, are basically a lot of good reviews of his celebrity and achievements.

Perhaps the most seductive, the most beguiling of narrative voice choices is that of the Innocent Narrator, like the boyish narrator of Frank McCourt's *Angela's Ashes*. The reader knows a boy didn't write the book—but a boy tells the story. The narrative voice is as innocent at nineteen as he is at three or four. Though I love Frank McCourt's book, for me this wistful voice begins to fray, to falter as the narrator enters his teens, especially after sex enters the story. *Angela's Ashes* is a story of class, country, religion, and poverty, but by invoking the persistently Innocent Narrator, the author, Frank McCourt, need never address those concepts by name, nor write the words alcoholism, desertion, humiliation, or poverty. In keeping his narrator a perpetual Innocent, the author counts on the adult reader to fill in a larger understanding of what the boy endured, the alcoholism, the humiliation, the grinding, grisly daily assaults on self-respect. The Innocent Narrator need not make judgments. The reader can do that. The reader *will* do that.

McCourt is so sophisticated a writer that he makes this ongoingly Innocent narrative voice look easy. It isn't. I once worked with a gifted writer who had fantastic powers of recollection. As a small child in wartime England, she could remember vividly events as early as age three. When she first began writing her memoir, she adhered so closely to that child's perspective that if the child didn't have the descriptive word for an object, the narrator would not use the noun. Case in point: The mother brings the little girl into a shop where she buys two ounces of tea. The clerk weighs the dry tea on a scale. But the three-year-old doesn't have the word for *scale*, and being absolutely true to that viewpoint, all she can do is describe the scale itself in all its various parts. This description was, as you might well imagine, tedious, and confusing, and it went on at boring length, bogging down not only the scene, but the entire story. When she revised, this writer relinquished her literal adherence to the child; she described the object as a scale, and life (and the memoir) went happily on.

Let's return briefly to Netta Gibbs's description of that family photo in the backyard with laundry flapping on the line. If she rendered that into an actual scene in her memoir (say, if she opened with it, to anchor the people who will be important to her memoir), how could she best present it? If her narrative voice stuck to the point of view of herself as a little child, her emphasis would need to be on the Mary Jane shoes and the lovely pink dress; that's where her childish attention was fastened. If she brings a more adult perspective, she can offer insight that little girl would not have. I've long thought that narrative voice was the true achievement of Harper Lee's *To Kill A Mockingbird*. It opens with an adult casting nostalgically back to her childhood, and then the story lounges around (figuratively speaking) in that town/family/neighborhood thirty years before without the reader ever quite realizing that the narrator has actually slid into the actual point of view of the kid, Scout, herself.

Every narrative voice carries with it certain restrictions, responsibilities. Sometimes you have to write a lot before those restrictions come clear. I worked for a long time with a writer who has a wonderful chronicle of an adventurous, pioneering childhood, homesteading in Alaska in the 1950s. He and his older brother were only four and five years old when the family first arrived in Valdez, Alaska, where his father was to be the pastor of a church not yet built. The elder brother, even as a little boy, was brave, eager for adventure, unafraid of mischief. The younger brother—that is, the writer—portrays himself throughout as the kid who wanted to stay home with Mom, who got tired and cold and hungry, the reluctant tag-along, not only not-brave, but the proverbial scaredy-cat. For all the dramatic contrast between the brothers, their shared, unshakable bond is one of the key themes of the book. After writing quite a lot, the author began to see that for the story he wanted to convey, keeping the whole in the voice and understanding of the little boy created some disconcerting dilemmas.

For one, pioneer life in Alaska required a lot of often complex procedures, like home-canning tons of just-caught salmon. (To say nothing of the expedition that his family and the kids and adults from a nearby orphanage all went on to catch that salmon!) Using a little-boy narrator, the author always needed to place an adult nearby to explain (in dialogue) these processes to the reader. This grew tedious and repetitive, and it slowed the pace. Another dilemma: the little boy's vocabulary was unequal to the majesty, the beauty, and the perils of Alaska. In later drafts this writer shook off the shackles of the boy. The kid remains the point of view, and he retains the narrator's essential character ("I wanna go home. I'm cold. I'm hungry. I'm tired . . ."), but the author freed his descriptive powers, broadened his vocabulary to do justice to the experience of his unique childhood.

Resist the temptation to make your narrator look too good, too knowing, too sophisticated. Let it be said up front and without equivocation that the narrator should not be a whiner (*Poor me . . . they were all so mean to me. . . . It wasn't my fault . . .* ). The superior narrator is always a bore (*Of course I could never believe such religious tripe, I always knew better . . .* ). The persistently self-justifying narrator is wearisome and predictable. The narrator who is the hero of every episode will not finally be heroic. Ironically, for a great example of how *not* to write a narrative voice, you have only to read Frank McCourt's brother, Malachi McCourt's, *Swimming With Monks*. Malachi, in my opinion, commits all these narrative faux pas. He portrays himself as the hero, swaggering through his story and justifying his every move and decision, including some that suggest questionable judgment, but never mind, he's always got a good reason, and he certainly has a lot of lively adventures. Increasingly, as the book goes on, however, the adventures pale and grow monotonous because they are persistently inflected with his own fine opinion of himself, unchanging. Reading that book is like being on a cross-country flight seated beside the biggest blowhard you can imagine.

———

In turning memory into memoir, there will be a transformation of the past. The author makes judgments about what to include, what to exclude; about how to tell the story so that the past is shaped into story, and not merely rendered as an onslaught of words (as in, say, First Things Fast). The author creates the voice that will inform that story. The voice that tells the story will alter the story that is told. If, say, you are describing a childhood accident from the immediate point of view of two kids fooling around with a chemistry set when it blows up, that perspective is very different from an adult's hard-won wisdom that the explosion would leave his brother with burns he would always carry, or take out an eye, or some other catastrophe.

To better understand how narrative voice can influence the story itself, look at the brief memoirs below. Eleanor Irving is telling the exact same story in each of them. They are each rooted in the same day when, at the age of four, her radical Communist parents took her to a Ban the Bomb march in 1957, and she met the famous scientist, activist, and Nobel Prize–winner, Linus Pauling (1901–1994). That's the story. But look how different is the tone of each! The tone changes not only the way the experience is conveyed, but the *truth implied* in the scene.

### A BLESSING IN WASHINGTON SQUARE

Dad followed Mom through the crowd with me perched on his shoulders at that Ban the Bomb march in Washington Square, October, 1957. "Join the Workingman's Union," my mother called out as she put leaflets into the hands of anyone who smiled at her.

My red hair stood out in the crowd. People would stop my dad, and ask how Little Red was doing. "I'm not little," I protested. "I'm Big Red." Mom and Dad laughed, and so did the marchers.

Threading through the crowd was an old man with wild hair and piercing blue eyes. He stopped in front of us, and smiled, reached up and shook my hand. My dad put me down on the ground and the old man touched my red curls in a light caress. He spoke, not to me, but seemingly addressed someone none of us could see. My mother bit her lips like she was going to cry.

"It's like being blessed by the Pope," my father whispered as the man left us and went up to the podium.

"Linus Pauling is better than the Pope," said Mom.

This chipper narrative voice keeps within the parameters of childhood. There's a sense of celebration conveyed in her description of the crowd. People are kind. Mom is smiling. They are Mom and Dad rather than the more formal "my parents." The Nobel Prize–winner Linus Pauling is just an "old guy with wild hair." The reader has to wait for Mom to identify him as a person of renown and respect (better than the Pope!). Mom and Dad recognized the honor when it was bestowed upon Eleanor; the youthful narrator did not.

LITTLE RED

My parents dragged me to every Ban the Bomb march and Workingman's Union rally from the time I was a babe in arms. When I was about four, Linus Pauling himself all but blessed me. My parents were not mere lily-livered Socialists, but card-carrying Commies in an era when that label could cost you. It did cost them, passionate as they were. They couldn't get jobs, or if they got them, they were soon fired. Never mind. My parents were happiest writing leaflets and rousing the faithful. Sometimes the very food we ate was donated. As for the rent, we moved sometimes twice a year. I always shared my bedroom with the mimeograph machine, and that odor is the strongest recollection of my childhood. People used to call me Little Red, as if that were my name. When I was thirteen I outright refused to go to any more meetings, or hand out any more leaflets. I told them, I'm through being Little Red. Find another poster child. My parents probably wanted to beat me, but they couldn't. It was against their principles.

In this version, the "blessing" by Linus Pauling is of almost no interest whatsoever to the narrator. There's little scenic depiction and no dialogue. There's certainly no joy in this description of what it meant to be Little Red, which is only mentioned when the narrator disavows the title. This narrator telescopes into the future, into Eleanor's adult estimation of her parents' lives and passions. This narrator renders her childhood experience through the prism of her adult resentment. The overall tone here is harsh bordering on bitter, so much so that in some ways it brings the whole scene, maybe even the whole memoir, to a halt.

## WASHINGTON SQUARE

Butcher, baker, Indian chief, they all crowded into Washington Square to a Ban the Bomb protest in October 1957 where Linus Pauling would be speaking. On my father's shoulders, I was the Little Red Princess, daughter of bona fide Radicals. We followed my mother through the crowd as she handed out Workingman's Union leaflets to bearded old men and babushka-clad grannies, to intense, fiery-eyed young students, and pale, overworked factory girls, to artists wearing paint-stained moth-eaten sweaters, and men with stumps where their hands ought to be and placards round their necks crying out for justice against capitalists who cared nothing for industrial accidents.

My father always reached in his pocket and gave these old men change, though God knows we ate nothing but pancakes or oatmeal for weeks at a time. The coat on my back, the shoes on my feet, were the gifts of people who admired my parents. How could they have had so little pride that they could accept charity from people scarcely better off than we were? What wouldn't they sacrifice for The Cause? My parents were proud to have been blacklisted, imprisoned, impoverished and yet remain true to their principles. Blubbering, blundering, oppressed humanity meant more to them than the well being of their children. That day in Washington

Square when Linus Pauling, stopped, reached out, and blessed me, for my parents that was the pinnacle of my life, of their lives.

Eleanor Irving opens here with a bright and lively scenic depiction of the march itself, and a wonderful sense of the crowd, though, to my mind, leaving Mom and the leaflets out is something of a loss. In paragraph two, she almost instantly forsakes that immediate moment in Washington Square. Eleanor alters the narrator's perspective and the voice changes to that of a knowing adult. She questions her parents' choices, their values, and she criticizes those choices and values. The blessing by Linus Pauling is, again, of almost no narrative interest; she doesn't even bother to describe it. She mentions it only to note that her parents thought it the pinnacle of their lives, and clearly (you can tell from the tone) Eleanor did not see it as the pinnacle of *her* life. This shift in perspective between paragraphs is jarring, and it interrupts any transition that will allow Eleanor to return her narrative to Washington Square, 1957. Hard to imagine where the memoir might go next.

## Combining Narrative Styles

Must the narrator remain consistent throughout? Not necessarily.

Maxine Kingston's nontraditional narrative voice in *The Woman Warrior* changes from chapter to chapter. Because these are memoir essays, she has the freedom to use all sorts of narrative voices, sometimes a dream-self who partakes in powerful imaginative adventures; elsewhere her narrative voice turns angry, sarcastic. The more traditional "I" narrator barely surfaces till late in the book, and shortly thereafter she flaunts her own lies to the reader. However, read together, and in order, though the narrative voice is not consistent, the essays create a kind of choral effect.

Here is Netta Gibbs with a different kind of voice than the one she created from First Things. In this short essay she mixes up her child's-eye view with adult perspective. She brings an adult's bemused sensibility to bear on her material, shifting smoothly from the adult's wry canopy insight to the kid's experience, and back again. Her shifts in perspective are gracefully transitioned.

## GRAN THEF OTTO

Delusion runs deep in my family. You can trace the strain of delusion like the blue eyes, or the family overbite, or weak ankles that I can see around the table every Thanksgiving. Our various houses were too small to accommodate all the assorted Gibbs and associates, so we usually went to my Great Aunt Anna's. Her sons lined up tables in the garage, and plugged in a few space heaters, and we all bundled up and celebrated amidst the hoses and tools hanging from the un-insulated walls. After dinner the men always went into the livingroom to watch football, and the women stayed in the kitchen. The older kids got put to work or were up to mischief. I was too young for mischief, but I knew better than to be underfoot.

One Thanksgiving I was left to dawdle with a particularly unpleasant little girl some three or four years my senior. I remember her dress, a maroon velvet with a lace collar, which I coveted. Let's just call her Samantha, a name that suits her long lovely curls, and her relish in malice. No doubt Samantha thought I would cry my eyes out when she snuggled up beside me and said my brother Joe was a jailbird and that he wasn't here this Thanksgiving because he was in the can serving time for Grand Thef Otto.

I had few tools to make sense of this, and she, Miss La-di-dah, having delivered her nasty news, sashayed off. What really bothered me was her coarse contempt (yes, an eight year old can have coarse contempt) for my absolutely insisting that Joe was in the Army stationed at Fort Dix. She left me to puzzle over what kind of time was Joe serving? And from what kind of can? Was he a waiter somewhere? And who was Gran Thef Otto, and why would Joe be with him?

Later that night I asked my mother who was Gran Thef Otto and if he was a relative like Great Aunt Anna. My mother's face relaxed into a smile. Yes. He was Great Aunt Anna's husband, Otto, who hadn't lived with her for years. He was far away. Like Joe, only not at Fort Dix. Mom thought he might be a cook on a fishing boat in Alaska.

A few months later I asked Great Aunt Anna how was Gran Thef Otto and when was he coming home to live with her again. Once she picked up the gist of the conversation, she patted my hand, and asked if I would I like an Oreo cookie, an offer guaranteed to take my attention from Gran Thef Otto and the past.

Anna, too, subscribed to the family delusion that any old scandal could be effectively wadded into a good story, thrown against the wall, and made to stick there. In fact, Anna's husband was named Wilbur, not Otto, and Wilbur too had gone to prison (forgery and attempted manslaughter) and while he was gone, Anna had two more children by two different men. And no one was ever the wiser.

As you move through drafts of your memoir, and get more material on the page, have a careful look at the overall voice you have used to tell the tale. Does the narrative perspective change between paragraphs like Eleanor Irving's, creating confusion? Is the narrator an Innocent, like Frank McCourt? An embittered adult? Is your narrator high-spirited like Mary Karr? Is your narrator casual, colloquial as Rick Bragg? The most important question to ask: Is your narrator equal to the task? As the author of the Alaska pioneer memoir discovered, once you recognize the narrative voice that your memoir needs, that moment will buoy your writer's heart for days, even weeks. Maybe years.

# 11 | Revising the Memoir

*"Here's the difference: you have to live your life,*
*but you get to revise your memoir."*
—Laura Kalpakian, *The Memoir Club*

D ear writer, imagine after a long day you close up your laptop, raise your weary, bleary eyes, and see before you three bottles. The first is marked "Well Done." Lift this bottle, and take a quick, bright swig. You got a lot of words down today! Pages written! Progress made! Hooray! Another bottle awaits nearby, this one marked "Could Do Better." And this you know to be true. So, with a bit of Humphrey Bogart's "Play it again, Sam," world-weary resignation, you lift that bottle and sip. But the third bottle? The one that's marked "That Sucked"? Avoid that one. Put the cork back in and push it to the side. To believe your work sucks will defeat you. To believe that every golden word is exactly where and how and what it ought to be, that delusion will equally defeat you. You need to retain your writerly equilibrium.

Revising is absolutely essential. Revising much and often. Revising sometimes ruthlessly. Revising to hold yourself artistically and editorially accountable. Revision should be understood as re-vision, to re-see, re-think, indeed, re-member—as in to break apart, and reassemble. Writing is a process until it has an ISBN number. Then the book is an artifact. Before that, your work is draft, and draft can be tinkered with, adjusted, revised, trimmed, expanded, enhanced, and enriched at will.

When to revise? In general revising ought to take place:

1. Daily (or every time you return to your writing).
2. Intermittently when you have amassed some material and now are seeking some larger structure to put over that narrative, to give it better shape or voice.

3. When you have what feels like the whole in hand, and you want to refine for clarity, grace, and style. This "whole" can be a book, or an essay, or a chapter, or something in between.

If you are making *major changes*, like a brand-new opener, say, save what you have *as is*, and start afresh with a different file. (Like Ch. 2 ALT for Alternate.) Save any material you cut. It may yet be useful.

## Revising Daily

One step forward, three steps back. Each time you return to your material, do not begin work where you left off. Going back to what you have already written helps you to wade into the material, the mood, to pick up momentum if you had it, to create momentum if you did not. How far back? Depends. On a daily working basis, I go back to the beginning. Not, I assure you, to page one of a four-hundred-page novel, but to the beginning of each chapter. Individual chapters are more easily managed, mentally and logistically. I always work in individual chapters; I do not combine them into the whole book till the very end of the process. Indeed, by the time you leave Chapter One to move on, you might well have discovered that the last few paragraphs of Chapter One are actually the beginnings of Chapter Two. Maybe you will have found that your current Chapter One isn't the beginning after all. So be it. Be resilient. Be open to where your material wants to go. I try to keep these drafts in folders with the month and year noted.

People often speak of writer's block, a phrase I dislike. Every writer at some point experiences that awful dead end where, try as you might, the story resists every effort to move forward. In that case, look behind you. The problem of the stubborn resistance of story—writer's block, if you like—does not lie ahead, it lies behind. The inability to move forward can be cured by going backward. (I have learned from experience.) The answer is behind you, waiting there, though veiled.

How to lift that veil?

*Early rounds of revision are for expansion.*

In the initial drafts, writers sometimes use the narrative equivalent of placeholders, something tucked in but not developed. Perhaps you have a narrative placeholder where actually a scene needs to be. Perhaps you have written in generalities, material that needs to be opened up, filled in with particulars. Perhaps a line or two of dialogue, in truth, needs to be a full exchange. Is there a place where you have a mere paragraph that begs to become a *scene*, complete with dialogue and detail? Perhaps what you initially think is backstory opens up and becomes revelatory

Consider a scene like this: your coworker returns from vacation.

"How was your vacation?"
"Great. I had a great time."
"Nice."

All very bland, boring, lacking all vigor, vitality, or detail.

But look what happens if, in revision, you ask questions that will eke out the particulars. What did you do? *I went.... [camping, fishing, sightseeing, hiking, to cooking class ... ]* Did you come home changed? *I came home with [a broken arm, a broken heart, a tattoo, a sunburn...]* Where was your best meal? The most memorable sight? The starriest sky? The sunniest day? The biggest wave? The funniest anecdote? The kindest stranger? Missed connections? Lost luggage? Any, all of these offer color, voice, brightness, and vivacity. In revising, go back and tease out of that placeholder what is lurking there.

In terms of development and expansion, remember that Frank McCourt's entire story in *Angela's Ashes* could have been told in perhaps fifty words about poverty, religion, Ireland, and drink. Instead, he's given us some four hundred and fifty pages (paperback edition) of wonderful scenes. One of my favorite scenes could have been a placeholder as simple as the narrator saying, "One November our family moved to an even more wretched lodging than where we lived in before. The common privy for the whole block was at our back door." Twenty-nine words. Informationally OK. But vivacity? No. Instead, in the book the McCourt family arrives at this squalid, smelly place. As they put their few belongings down, Dad tries to make the best of where they find themselves; Mom is sullen; the boys are tired and hungry. A man comes to the back and dumps his chamber pot into the privy. Mrs. McCourt angrily demands to know how dare he dump his chamber pot in their privy! The man laughs as he leaves: Their privy! Ha ha ha. This is the privy for the whole block, and if you think it stinks now in November, Missus, just wait till June!

And that vivid scene is how the reader knows the McCourts have sunk into yet deeper squalor than they even imagined.

———

For examples of placeholders and the possibilities of expansion, let's return to Eleanor Irving's short, intense, embittered paragraph that basically slammed her memoir into a wall.

## LITTLE RED

My parents dragged me to every Ban the Bomb march and Workingman's Union rally from the time I was a babe in arms. When I was about four, Linus Pauling himself all but blessed me. My parents were not mere lily-livered Socialists, but card-carrying Commies in an era when that label could cost you. It did cost them, passionate as they were. They couldn't get jobs, or if they got them, they were soon fired. Never mind. My parents were happiest writing leaflets and rousing the faithful. Sometimes the very food we ate was donated. As for the rent, we moved sometimes twice a year. I always shared my bedroom with the mimeograph machine, and that odor is the strongest recollection of my childhood. People used to call me Little Red, as if that were my name. When I was thirteen I outright refused to go to any more meetings, or hand out any more leaflets. I told them, I'm through being Little Red. Find another poster child. My parents probably wanted to beat me, but they couldn't. It was against their principles.

In her headlong rush to stand wholly apart from her parents' values and beliefs, Eleanor used her narrative voice as an angry megaphone, but she deprived her story of depth, and she left readers wondering at her passion. In revising let's look at the places where her material cries out for development. Let's ask questions about what is here, and indeed, what is not.

*My parents dragged me to every Ban the Bomb march and Workingman's Union rally from the time I was a babe in arms. When I was about four, Linus Pauling himself all but blessed me.*

Linus Pauling! Tell us about that, Eleanor. The Nobel Prize–winner! A two-time Nobel Prize–winner? Moreover, there may be readers who never heard of Linus Pauling. His importance needs to be established. What does he mean that he "blessed" you? Did he put his hand on your head and look heavenward? What happened?

*My parents were not mere lily-livered Socialists, but card-carrying Commies in an era when that label could cost you. It did cost them, passionate as they were. They couldn't get jobs, or if they got them, they were soon fired.*

Tell us something more about this era in which being a card-carrying Commie could hurt you. Why? How? What kind of jobs did they have? Why were they fired?

*Never mind. My parents were happiest writing leaflets. . . . I always shared my bedroom with the mimeograph machine, and that odor is the strongest recollection of my childhood. . . .*

You remember the smell of the mimeograph machine, what about the leaflets themselves? What were they about? Titles? Contents?

*As for the rent, we moved sometimes twice a year.*

Did you stay in the same neighborhoods? Apartments? Houses? Duplexes? Did your living situation deteriorate? What was the best living situation you ever had? What was the worst?

*And rousing the faithful.*

What does it mean to rouse the faithful, Eleanor? Did they have public meetings like in a church or a union hall? Or did they stand on the street and hand out tracts and berate the capitalists? Were they freelance Commies? Oh, there's no such thing as a freelance Commie? OK. To whom did they answer? What were these other Communists like? Authoritarian doctrinaires, or lively, spirited debaters? Or both? Or neither? Who were these people, and how did they fit into your life, your parents' lives, their work?

*Sometimes the very food we ate was donated.*

By whom? Other like-minded radicals? Social workers? Government programs? What did you eat? Were you chronically short of food?

*When I was thirteen I outright refused to go to any more meetings, or hand out any more leaflets. I told them, I'm through being the Little Red Princess. Find another poster child.*

You repudiated the life and the values they had raised you to cherish. Why at age thirteen? Did something happen at thirteen that set you off, soured you on all that they stood for, or was it teenage rebellion? What was their response? Was there an argument? Voices raised? Tears? Threats?

*My parents probably wanted to beat me, but they couldn't. It was against their principles.*

Even if they couldn't beat you, Eleanor, was there a price to pay? What was that price? How did it affect the rest of your youth? The rest of your life?

Clearly, taking out Eleanor's placeholders and expanding on them will open up the narrative, possibly into a book, certainly well beyond this angry paragraph. In the process of expanding we would, I believe, see something of the evolution of Eleanor's feelings about her parents, about the Communists and their ideals. In effect, she would tell us not simply what she learned (to detest her parents' values), as her original paragraph does, but how she learned it.

INTERIM REVISION

Any piece of narrative prose has to find its method of telling. Fundamentally, what you want to discover as you write is the core organizing principle you can use as a sort of spindle for your whole story, whether that is a book, or an essay, or a series of memoir essays. Sometimes the structure comes to the author in a wonderful flash of conviction. Sometimes the author has to Braille through a hundred pages of draft to find out how the story ought to be told. Should it be chronologically a la *Angela's Ashes* or *Up From Slavery*? Thematically arranged essays a la *Notes of a Native Son*? Anthony Bourdain organizes *Kitchen Confidential* like a formal meal from Appetizer to Dessert and Coffee and a Cigarette. In Patricia Volk's charming memoir of her restaurant-owing family, *Stuffed*, the chapters about various family members are named for certain dishes, Chopped Liver, Meat Loaf. For some memoirs the organizing principle is right there in the title: *Eat, Pray, Love*. Any memoir you read, ask yourself: What is the core organizing principle here?

Sometimes the material itself will dictate how the story gets told. A memoir that describes the journey of recovery can start with the narrator well and healthy and follow her spiral into illness or addiction. Or, such a memoir could first establish some terrible moment in the depths of illness or addiction, and then flash back to the beginning. Would such a story start in the *middle* of a downward spiral? No. The reader needs to know how desperate the narrator was, or, by contrast, from whence she fell. In Dani Shapiro's *Inheritance*, she swiftly describes the process of discovery, learning that her late, beloved father was not her actual biological father. The *implications* of that discovery are the subject of the book, not the detective work. Maxine Kingston's masterful structure of the essays in *The Woman Warrior* reveals slowly that her mother, Brave Orchid, is truly the heroine here. And in Vladimir Nabokov's *Speak Memory*, the father—his life and death—emerge as the spindle around which these essays are subtly spun. (As in one of Nabokov's classic stories, the key is the ringing telephone.) In organizing your memoir essays remember that the information your reader has access to will accrue, so you don't want to repeat yourself. You'll want to order them so that they build toward a dramatic climax, or so that they have a rhythm.

Sometimes revising will move your material into uncharted waters. Linda Morrow began writing her memoir, *The Heart of This Family*, to chronicle the struggles she faced as the mother of a son, Steve, born with Down syndrome in 1966. At that time there were no educational structures for these children, and most were institutionalized. Linda refused to do this. In advocating for her son, for his education, Linda crashed through many barriers, celebrated small triumphs, and endured much heartbreak and many setbacks. When she started writing her memoir in 2012, she began chronologically: Steve's birth followed by the births of two more sons, and the family's various relocations. However, she was never sure where or how the story ought to end, or how much of her own life she ought to include; in short, after writing for a couple of years she had a lot of pages, but the structure remained unclear. At the suggestion of a developmental editor, Linda's late revisions moved beyond her original intent, addressing emotions and challenges she hadn't planned to write about. The book opened up beyond Steve's boyhood to include chapters about the breakdown of her marriage, the discovery of her own true self, and a new partnership forged with the woman who later became her wife. *The Heart of This Family* now follows Steve into adulthood, the story bracketed, beginning and ending, with crucial events in 2015.

As Linda's experience suggests, to truly discover the spindle for the structure of your memoir, you need to have amassed some pages. As Peggy Kalpakian Johnson wrote *Centennial Memoir*, the subtitle, *A Tribute to My Parents*, provided her with the core organizing principle. She wanted her book to recognize, honor her parents' bravery in emigrating to the United States, their struggles and successes in becoming American. Once she knew that, the structure clarified.

*Chapter 1 The Old Country (1915 to 1922)*
*Chapter 2 The Journey (1923)*
*Chapter 3 The New Country (1923 to 1940)*

But as she wrote, created more draft, other stories came to her, stories that didn't always fit into this neat chronological/geographical presentation. Grace Towner, the teacher who saved my grandmother's life in Adana, Turkey, needed her own chapter. The horrors that Haigouhi's little brother endured in the desert required a singular chapter. These and other new elements, each in some way, contributed to the core principle, but they would not fit into simple chronology or geography. As a writer Peggy was resilient, attentive to the needs of her narrative, and following Chapters 1, 2, and 3 she added new chapters, rounding out the larger picture of her immigrant family's experience in America, including recipes and Armenian names and phrases. She ended the book with a chapter called Farewells, telling the lives of her late sisters, the last of whom had died in 2016.

The poster child of What Not to Do in terms of structure is Havelock Ellis's *My Life: Autobiography of Havelock Ellis*. Ellis (1859–1939) is almost totally forgotten now, a footnote at the edges of important intellectual and artistic currents. But in his era he was famous. He was known as a "sexologist" and he outraged Victorians and Socialists alike—and not just with his writings. His autobiography ought to have been juicy reading. But on the page each time he meets or introduces some louche, bohemian companion, he pauses there and goes on to describe his entire relationship with that person, wandering well in advance of the story, ending often with that person's death. This structure renders his book dolorous. When he returns to the events originally under discussion, the thread has been broken, and rather than finding his life an account of salty adventures, and lively encounters, the reader feels as if she is sitting at some perpetually somber memorial service. His structure turns out to be a form of Narrative Ketchup.

Narrative Ketchup is the great foe of a smoothly structured narrative. Narrative Ketchup happens when you introduce information that takes you far afield from what you have been developing. Narrative Ketchup happens when you suddenly stop your chapter or paragraph or sentence and *Catch Up!*, halt your original scene in order to stop and clarify. The depth and momentum you have built up dissipates, and the narrative derails. You can sadly sabotage your own structure with these splashes of Narrative Ketchup.

Annie was my best friend in the Kansas City. We did everything together. We met singing in the Baptist church choir when we were twelve. Annie went to London in '68 and for a while she shacked up with one of Herman's Hermits. She had two kids and a bad cocaine addiction. She lived in Wimbledon for years, but returned home to Kansas City a couple of years ago to . . .

We ran out of gas in the middle of the desert because the gas gauge quit working two weeks before when I told Chris he had to fix it, but no, he . . .

We moved Daddy to a nursing home after he'd been sick for a long time. My mom had noticed the year before that he had trouble breathing, wheezing a lot and he got tired easily and his short term memory was shot. She took him to the doctor who sent him to the neurologist who. . . .

My brother, Will, hit me with his cast and I bellowed in pain. Will had broken his arm in a football accident in October when in the last few minutes of the second quarter, he ran into the goal post while making a touchdown . . .

When you find yourself writing long asides like the ones implied above, stop. Question your information. Ask yourself, where does it really belong? What context do you need to supply *in advance* so that your action scene or thought or dramatic moment can be delivered in a way that is indeed active or thoughtful or dramatic? What information needs to be moved so that you can linger and develop the scene where you *want* to lavish your narrative attention? Ask yourself, how can I integrate this material into the whole? Indeed, does it need to be integrated? Or is it rather superfluous? Does it need its own paragraph? Its own chapter?

The more you write, these questions will start to resolve themselves as the story begins to fill in and fill out.

## LATER ROUNDS OF REVISION

Returning to your draft late in the process, you want to revise for clarity, grace, and style.

CLARITY means readers never have to stop and say, What? What's happening here? Who is under discussion? What did I just read and what does it mean? Who is speaking here? Where is this taking place?

STYLE means your readers never have to stop because they're bored or unengaged, or that your transitions are so rocky that readers get lost between paragraphs, that readers find your material dull, repetitive, or vague.

GRACE suggests that your work rewards readers with a pleasurable experience, introduces them to events, people, ideas outside their own lives and contexts rendered in prose that is compelling, even memorable. Grace incorporates writing that is fresh, sprightly, lively, that can convey both atmosphere and action. In short, writing that creates a sort of enchantment.

The question that will help you achieve these aims is a simple one. As you read you ask yourself, *does this* (title, opening, scene, dialogue exchange, etc.) *serve the narrative?*

If the answer is no, then cut, or connect, or condense, or expand, enrich, or somehow alter so that it *does* serve the narrative. Everything you have on the page has to serve the narrative.

Some specifics:

TITLES: Always work with a title, however temporary. Having a title is like a having a compass through the wilderness, even if you change the title often. I have written books that kept the same title from the time I picked up the pen until it was in print years later. And then, there have been those like *The Great Pretenders* (2019) that had half a dozen titles while it was in draft, including for a while the utterly generic The

Hollywood Novel. Not until late in the process did I stumble on the canopy thematic, *The Great Pretenders*. So, even if your title is makeshift, and you change it many times, having a title will help focus your material. If you do change the title, then you must go back and weave the thematic implicit in the new title through the whole. Each chapter should have a title too, even if you later remove it, and just leave them numbered.

OPENING: Why is this (chapter, scene, paragraph, sentence) the beginning? Make your opener (chapter, scene, or paragraph) atmospheric so that the reader is pulled in. No matter how wonderful your subsequent chapters, if your opener is weak, no reader will willingly continue.

DIALOGUE: Dialogue reveals character and conveys mood and information, and ascribing dialogue to a character automatically endows them with importance. However, as a primary narrative device, it's not always efficient or economical, especially if people blather on, claiming narrative space on the page, but accomplishing little or nothing in terms of forwarding the story or creating tension.

To edit your dialogue, pull it from the rest of that section or chapter and look at it *on its own*. No supporting material. Study it for infelicities, tired exchanges, or material that essentially repeats info already given. Do you stop after every quote mark to tell us what's going on with the character's face or nose or eyebrows? Get rid of that stuff. Look at adverbs. If they refer to voice or tenor of voice (he said angrily . . . ) then have a serious look at the words you have used in the exchange itself. How can you strengthen that speech so as to *convey* the anger (or any emotion) rather than use an adverb to color it? Ask yourself, does the dialogue deepen understanding of your characters, their actions and choices? Does it propel the story? Does it flow? If one character is asked a question, the answer must follow. Otherwise, people are not talking *to each other*, they are simply squawking lines.

In general (and this is important), most dialogue can be condensed and connected for dramatic efficiency. After your first few drafts, look at it and see where you can combine speeches so that characters' dialogue is richer, more informative, rewarding, and nonredundant. Avoid long pages of one-liners.

CHARACTER PORTRAYAL: Characters in memoir and fiction grow, become vivid by making choices. Have you given your characters opportunity to do so? Have you moved your characters through the landscapes you've created, be they kitchens or classrooms, canning salmon, or handing out Communist leaflets? Did you introduce a character, lavish time, care, and dialogue on them, and *not* develop that individual? If so, develop or diminish accordingly. Margo Jefferson in *Negroland* uses an interesting technique to address this difficulty. For those people who will only show up ephemerally in her story, she introduces them with only initials, rendering them immediately into bit players. This technique frees her narrator to concentrate on the characters she wants to develop and the story she wants to tell in her nontraditional memoir.

Does your memoir grow tedious by constantly describing people in terms of their relationship to the narrator? My grandmother . . . my cousin . . . my mother. . . . Are there places where you can portray these people with their *names*, free them, so to speak, from their bondage to the narrator? If you are writing about Mom, remember she wasn't always Mom. Before she was Mom, she was someone else; use her correct name, at least until she becomes Mom. Endowing "Mom" and "Dad" with their real names when possible gives them dimension as individuals in their own right.

SCENIC PORTRAYAL: Is *each* of your scenes vivid? Can readers imagine the world in which this memoir takes place? The light, the noise, scents and sensory considerations, the weather, physical comforts or discomforts? Is this info in the right place? Does it need to be better sifted? Is it repetitive?

Can you condense for effect and economy? Is each scene connected to the one that comes before and the one that comes after, transitioned visually or thematically?

TRANSITIONS: Do your paragraphs transition smoothly, one to the next? Can you combine or condense some of them so as to evade the Department of Redundancy Department?

GET RID OF NARRATIVE SLUDGE: Junky, nonspecific phrases (especially prepositional phrases and lots of "it" and "there" phrases) that clutter and add no depth or meaning or info. If your characters are dressed in one scene and naked right after, they should probably take off their clothes. However, you, dear writer, do not need to close every door, wipe every tear, lift every fork, swallow every bite, place every glass on the bar, nor sugar every cup of tea. Too much of this slows your narrative to a crawl.

BURN UNNECESSARY BRIDGES: Sometimes you need a "bridge" in order to enter your material in the first place. Sometimes the bridge might be several paragraphs, even a few pages. The bridge can be as simple as "I remember when . . ." After you have arrived at what you remember, you no longer need "I remember when . . ." As a bridge, it's useless. Take it out, and plunge your reader into what you remember. Bridges that need burning are generally found at the beginnings.

VERB TENSES: In early drafts, very often your verb tenses will slide around. While you are drinking from the bottle marked "Well Done!" that's fine. Once you sip from "Could Do Better," be more critical. Try to keep verb tenses consistent throughout, unless, of course, you are altering or interspersing present and past tense for dramatic effect.

Present tense can be sprinkled in to the past tense to underscore drama, but if you have written the whole piece in present tense, perhaps rethink your choice. In the short-form essay, it can work well, but over the course of an entire book, present tense can become static, stale. Long tracts of present tense can drain tension, as though nothing is ever going to happen, nothing is ever going to change. (That said, I have to admit *Angela's Ashes* is wholly in the present tense.)

CRUCIAL: Any change you make—truly, any change—will reverberate through the whole. Any changes will require you to return and finesse through what you have written, both what came before and what comes after.

## Reading Like a Writer

To be a creative writer, you must also learn to be a creative reader; that is to say, you learn to read like a writer. To read like a writer means you continually ask the writerly questions of whatever is in your hand, be it a Pulitzer Prize–winning novel, or the work of someone in your writers' group. You will come to your reading experience with what are—eventually—reflexive questions. *Why is this the opener? How is this important? How did she create that effect? How did it work? Why did it work? (Or conversely, why does it not work?)* Reading like a writer is a skill that will not come to you overnight, but over time. However, once you do learn to read in this fashion, I'm sad to say you can never return to that headlong joy you felt as a kid plunging into *Anne of Green Gables,* or Roald Dahl books, or *Harry Potter.* This loss of reader innocence is an occupational hazard of learning how to read creatively, to revise creatively, in short, to write.

## A Very Quick Guide to Good Writing, Or: How to Trim, Polish, Tighten, and Enliven Your Prose

### THE FOOD CHAIN

In good writing there is a food chain. At the top of the chain is the *Verb.* Verbs literally make your prose move, give it life and vivacity. Strive always for the brilliant, the evocative verb. Think of all the ways there are simply to walk, and what these various ways might imply of the personality or emotional or physical state of the character. Rely on strong verbs and stay away from weak, inexpressive ones.

Right below the verb is the *Noun*, the proverbial person, place, or thing. Nouns have girth and grit and substance; they have weight and vivacity.

*Adjectives and Adverbs as Modifiers* are useful tools to the writer, but beware of strings of them. Better to choose a single lively verb than a bevy of adjectives or adverbs. For example, "He walked slowly down the street in a leisurely fashion" could be cleaner, more vivid and concise as, "He ambled down the street." "He strolled down the street." Do not rely on adjectives and adverbs to convey the underlying quality of your scene. "The sunset was lovely, the clouds were all red and rosy, and the full moon was just barely evident." This weak wording can be tweaked to: "The full moon peeked under reams of rosy clouds as dusk fell."

On the food chain, beneath the Modifiers are *Prepositions*. (The preposition is anything you can do to a little red wagon—well, almost anything. You can get on or under, in or over, etc.) Do not use more than two prepositional phrases in a row, three at the max. Your prose will become mechanical and develop a clanking quality with the likes of: "He came swiftly *through* the door and *across* the room *over* to the window." Better to say: "He crossed the room swiftly to the window." The preposition will always require an object, a noun like the door, the room, and the window.

At the very bottom of the food chain are the *Trash Can Words*, empty words and phrases, empty pronouns with no definite meaning. Like trash cans these words must have other words put into them in order to function. Chief among these is "it." Do not oblige these two flimsy letters to carry weight they are not equal to. Get rid of "It was Tom who ran the fastest race." No. "Tom ran the fastest race." Change "It was you who kept the family afloat." No. "You kept the family afloat." Never write: It is clear. Or, It is obvious. Or, It is anything else. Clearly. Obviously. When using "it" as an actual pronoun, be certain that the correspondence to the noun is clear. Ditto for the

Trash Can Word "thing." Ditto for the words "these," "this," and "those." Do not use them as pronouns. "This is why we . . ." No. Use them to modify nouns, such as "These ideas," "This notion," or "Those coincidences . . ." Doing so will oblige you to clarify your thoughts.

## AVOID THE PASSIVE VOICE

Passive voice: The child's lunch was made by me. (Note the preposition, "by," and the substitution of the object, the lunch, for the subject of the sentence ["me"].)

Active voice: I made the child's lunch. (I am the one *engaged in action*, making the child's lunch.)

The classic use of passive voice to evade responsibility is the expression, "Mistakes were made." Note that no one is taking credit or responsibility for those mistakes. A world of difference between that sentence, and "I made mistakes."

Along those lines, be certain that the grammatical subject of your sentence is in fact the *subject* of your sentence. For instance, look at the difference:

*It boggles the mind.*

Here the actual subject of the sentence is the trash can word "it," while the "mind," a noun, is left as the sort of handmaiden to the weak word.

*The mind boggles.*

Here, in fact, the *mind* boggles! And the mind is the actual, grammatical subject of the sentence!

Whenever possible do not begin a sentence with "There is . . ." for the same reason noted above. "There is a saying a long time ago . . ." (the weak, untethered, nonspecific there) becomes the grammatical subject and verb. Change to: "Long ago people said . . ."

## PARAGRAPHS AND SENTENCES

Develop your paragraphs. Strings of short choppy paragraphs will give your prose a lurching quality. Don't start out with one thought, but then wander off to other topics. Make certain that you haven't tried to do too much in one paragraph. Check your paragraphs for smooth transition from one to the next as you move down the page.

Vary your sentences in terms of structure and length. Avoid starting time after time with subject/verb. (*Mary went* to the store. *She bought* milk and eggs. *She paid* cash.) Or any structure that repeats continually. Rhythmically you lull your reader into a stupor. Use punctuation carefully. Too many exclamation points give your work a breathless rah-rah quality. Too many dashes can create a sense that the narrative is disjointed. Use of parentheses (always and automatically) shifts the narrative voice to a lower register.

———

Thank you to Mr. Sam Feldman for impressing these truths upon his high school journalism students and berating us when we failed to live up to them.

# 12 | Now What?

*"The act of memory is an act of will.*
*Like any such act of will, it obliges choices."*
—Penny Taylor in *The Memoir Club*, Laura Kalpakian

You have laughed and cried while you wrote your memoir. You have refined and revised and combed through the pages time and time again. You have struggled with structure and narrative voice, how to tell the tale. Perhaps you have shared portions of your memoir with close friends, or a writing group over time, or with some beta readers who have offered thoughtful suggestions. Perhaps you have worked with a developmental editor to bring out the best in your material. Your vignettes have evolved into episodes that have become essays; the essays have evolved into chapters. The chapters are looking like an actual book. Return to it, revise (again), tweak, pull, tug. Behold! It *is* an actual book! What do you do with it now?

For starters, you should think about placing some of your memoir essays, or some of your chapters, as stand-alone pieces in literary journals, anthologies, and other venues, online or print. You'll have to do some editing to be certain the piece *can* stand alone in terms of clarity, but that work is well worth the effort. The phrase "creative nonfiction" opens to a wide embrace, including, unless otherwise stated, memoir. Most literary journals will carry a judicious mix of literary forms, fiction, poetry, creative nonfiction, and memoir. Maxine Hong Kingston published the memoir essays in *The Woman Warrior* in journals before the book ever appeared, as did Vladimir Nabokov's *Speak, Memory*.

Of course one might correctly point out that Kingston and Nabokov were publishing in an era long removed from ours. Though that golden age of magazine pieces has indeed passed, online publishing opportunities abound. There are so many contemporary literary journals, especially online, that they are often fractured into social or political niches, and they only publish within those pickets, or perhaps they only publish within one genre. Some are geographically insulated, accepting work from writers either living in or associated with a certain locale, even an enormous locale, like the Pacific Northwest. Some will have special dedicated issues that explore specific questions. Alumni magazines (a flourishing market) will often have an end page that features a look to the past. Peggy Kalpakian Johnson published "Sunshine and Shadow," her essay about being a usc student during World War II, in the usc alumni magazine two years before her book came out. Even the most stately of literary journals (I think of *Ploughshares, Iowa Review, Prairie Schooner, Kenyon Review, Virginia Quarterly Review,* and so on) have an online presence. Memoir essays appearing in literary journals or anthologies can give the author a nice set of credentials when you go to find a publisher for your book, and of course it's always gratifying to see your name in print, even if online it lacks the smell of ink

Anthologies will call for submissions, usually on a particular topic. When Cami Ostman and Susan Tive put together *Beyond Belief: The Secret Lives of Women in Extreme Religions,* the work of first-time authors shared the Table of Contents page with writers who had national reputations. Sometimes writers' cooperatives will put out their own anthologies, providing editing services that would otherwise cost a good deal of money. How to discover these calls for submission? Again, the Internet can be a swamp of information, but a long-established outlet like *Poets and Writers* is a fine place to start. *Poets and Writers* has a print subscription, an online venue, and a free daily email. For a sense of the current publishing climate, *Writer's Digest,* a long-established forum, also has a lively online presence. Writers should also be familiar with the service Submittable, a sort of portal for submitting your work across many venues, magazines, competitions, and contests. Additionally, Submittable will help you keep track of these entries. Generally speaking, you can offer the same piece to more than one magazine or anthology for inclusion.

They ask only that you inform them and withdraw your work if it is to be published elsewhere.

## The Book

But what about the smell of fresh print? What about the actual, physical artifact of a book held in one's hand?

For some two hundred years American publishing was a staid, decorous "gentleman's" profession firmly established in Boston and New York. These fine houses disdained those little outlying presses that advertised discreetly in the prim side-columns of *The New Yorker*, presses that would publish writers for a fee—vanity presses, as they were termed. Then, twenty-some years ago, whoosh! That insular superiority was swept away! To be or become a publisher, one no longer needed a big, clunking press and a team of ink-stained printers to run it. One no longer needed a New York skyscraper office, nor a view of the Boston Common. Publishing was suddenly open to anyone with a computer, an Internet connection, some formatting capisce, marketing savvy, and access to a distributor. The e-book and the proliferation of e-book readers in the early 2000s meant you didn't even need to create a physical object.Gone is the benighted term *vanity press*. Even the term *self-publishing* has an archaic ring; these presses now come under the moniker of "indies" with its whiff of upstart irreverence. The quality of the services provided by these indies varies widely. A book badly bungled tarnishes the author's work, but many produce handsome artifacts, printed, proofed, designed with care, and if these titles are not reviewed in the *New York Times*, what of it? The book exists; the writer has become an author. Indie authors can join the Author's Guild, members in good standing with full privileges to all their many estimable services. And let us not forget that none other than Virginia and Leonard Woolf started their own press, Hogarth Press, an admirable indie if ever there was one.

In what seems to me an ironic return to eighteenth-century London when booksellers were often also publishers, writers may find that their local independent bookstore offers publishing services. Our local bookstore, Village Books, has two publishing tracks through which they have brought to fruition nearly two hundred books. They have their own Chuckanut Editions, as well as services to help authors publish under their own imprints. In each case the consignment cost for authors (the fee the bookstore takes to place it on the shelves) is less than they charge other indie authors, and the author has a venue in which to launch the book and where it will be featured prominently in the Local Authors display.

For an investment of time and money writers can absolutely see their work into print of some sort or another, sans agent, or even sans editor (though having no editor can be risky). How much time and how much money? That depends. Hydra-headed Amazon offers a labyrinth of publishing services. Some indie business models require that the author herself contracts separately with a designer, a proofer, and other individuals to create a book that will then come out under an independent banner. Some provide these services, though marketing and getting reviewed can be difficult problems. Certainly the author can market and sell her book wherever she likes (trade shows, professional conventions, book clubs, etc.), but the average indie will not have a publicity department to support these efforts. (An independent publicist can always be hired.) Some indies have banded together and have created their own trade shows and awards ceremonies, creating whole communities of readers and writers. For the writer for whom time is of the essence, the indie publisher is the answer. For a writer like Linda Morrow, in her early eighties when she finished her book, Sidekick Press had the finished volume in her hand within six months. And honestly, for a writer, there is no better feeling: to see thoughts that were in your head, there, in print, in your hand, that is a tremendous, never-to-be-forgotten rush. Truly, memory into memoir!

Another venue for the writer is hybrid publishing. Here the author contracts only with the publisher, and the house provides necessary services that a major house would: jacket design, book design, proofing, distribution, and marketing. The author pays an (often fat) fee but shares in the royalties. Hybrid publishers curate what they will offer. Some have wide distribution; their books get reviewed in well-known print and online outlets. Writers of my acquaintance who have gone with these firms have had good, though costly, experiences.

Many university presses are broadening their lists and offerings beyond the usual scholarly tomes, publishing poetry, fiction, creative nonfiction, and memoir. Sometimes these selections have a geographical affiliation to the press or the local population. Sometimes not. Paula Becker, a Washington author, published her heartbreaking memoir, *A House on Stilts: Mothering in the Age of Opioid Addiction*, with the University of Iowa Press. To have a sense of which university presses are seeking creative works in addition to their scholarly lists, have a look at the website of the Association of University Presses.

Traditional publishing where the author finds an agent who offers the work, sells it to a big corporate house, oversees foreign and dramatic rights, and takes fifteen percent of anything the author makes, is another possible avenue toward print. Seismic changes in traditional publishing over, say, the last thirty years have irrevocably altered the book-world landscape. Houses once independent (like those fronting the Boston Common) have been absorbed by the big corporations, who themselves have been absorbed by even bigger international corporations, so that now traditional publishing is mostly under the canopy of what's known as the Big Five. (And as of this writing, there's every indication that may well soon be the Big Four.) Under these canopies numerous imprints abound. The editors move around, sometimes by choice, sometimes made redundant as the houses merge imprints or slough them off. Pity the poor author whose *relationship* is with the editor, but whose *contract* is with the house. If the editor moves to another house or imprint, or is let go amid a restructure, the author can find her book orphaned with no champion in sight. (I speak from experience.) A relationship like F. Scott Fitzgerald's career-long association with one editor, Max

Perkins, at a family-owned house, Charles Scribner's Sons, is, for all intents and purposes, a thing of the past. Charles Scribner's Sons itself, founded in the nineteenth century, has been subsumed by the Big Five. In addition to the Big Five, there are a handful of particularly outstanding small presses like Graywolf, Melville House, Tin House, Coffee House Press, Milkweed, Copper Canyon, and, in California, Heyday Books. (Rock star Linda Ronstadt, who could no doubt have her pick of publishers, will bring out her book about her Mexican roots with Heyday.) These publishers offer great prestige to balance their miniscule advances. Be forewarned: most advances are miniscule in any event.

Seeking an agent to shepherd your work through this miasma can feel like a full-time job, hours spent poking about the Internet looking amid myriad websites. That said, the Internet means that literary agencies are far more transparent than they used to be. Do your homework: only query one person per agency or publishing house. There are online sites and classes that can help you in this search, including help creating that elusive thing so beloved of publishers called "platform." Embarking on this sort of journey will require a lot of time, many cups of coffee to sustain you, and probably a few beers to cry into for comfort.

## The Query Letter and Synopsis

Seeking an agent or any sort of publisher for your book requires a query letter and a synopsis of your book. Writing these two documents is the most difficult work you will ever have undertaken, including, if applicable, your dissertation; including, if applicable, the Dear John to your college boyfriend. Including the memoir you just finished.

Any agency will ask for a synopsis of your book. In my opinion, to offer a full synopsis as part of your inquiry is foolhardy and self-defeating. What you want to send is a lively description, the equivalent of flap copy, those enticing few paragraphs on the back of the paperback or the flaps of the hardcover: about five hundred words that make the bookstore browser want to cough up his money immediately.

Here is the difference between synopsis and flap copy:

SYNOPSIS: A girl lives in the forest with her mother who sews her a beautiful red cloak. Everyone calls her Little Red Riding Hood. Her grandmother, who lives in another part of the forest, gets sick, or at least the mother hasn't heard from her in a while, and so, fears she's sick. She sends LRRH through the woods with a basket for the grandmother. LRRH goes through the woods. She comes to the grandmother's house. Grandma is in bed, cowering under the covers. LRRH is worried. She puts her basket down and approaches Granny, wondering first at Granny's big eyes. Granny soothes her, though Granny's voice sounds funny. LRRH is worried, but she reasons that Granny's sick. She asks after Granny's ears when Granny rolls over, pulling the cover away, and the little girl sees Granny's big teeth! Oh no! Granny is not Granny at all! It's the Big Bad Wolf, and he has eaten Granny, and taken her place! LRRH goes into deep shock, but realizes quickly that she hasn't time to mourn dear Granny, BBW is coming after her too. Drooling. LRRH bolts for the door, but BBW beats her to it, and flings himself across it. His fangs gleam in the afternoon light. LRRH ducks and runs around the cabin screaming her bloody guts out with BBW bounding after her, still wearing Granny's night-dress. LRRH grabs a fireplace poker to defend herself, but BBW is too strong for her. BBW flings the poker aside, grabs LRRH, and opens his fierce jaws just as the door smashes open, and suddenly an axe thwacks BBW a mortal blow to his back. A nearby woodsman had heard LRRH's screams and came to her rescue. BBW lies in a bloody heap at her feet. LRRH, stunned, is comforted by the woodsman who accompanies her home through the woods. LRRH and her mother, though grieving for

Granny, are so grateful to him they give him the blackberry jam intended for her late grandmother.

OPENING LINE FOR FLAP COPY: Little Red Riding Hood braves the perils of the forest, only to arrive at her destination and find her grandmother mortally ill, and strangely beset by phantoms. Or demons. Will she share her grandmother's grisly fate? A tale of tested courage.

*Remember in describing your book: story is all and allure is everything.*

Flap copy requirements:

Highlight the central characters; cast the conflict, drama, and tension in compelling language.

Every sentence must be poignant, pungent, and fulfill all the above criteria.

No weak wording. No strings of prepositions, or tired phrases; no clichés.

Short paragraphs. Present tense.

Flap copy alludes to the setup, never the dénouement, though it can suggest a shattering ending.

Flap copy is not necessarily chained to the sequence of events as they appear in the book.

Flap copy must be grammatically perfect. Any stupid errors will condemn you to rejection.

Keep in mind the ongoing Big Questions: Whose story is it? What's at stake?

Let's return to *The Great Gatsby*. Imagine that you are F. Scott Fitzgerald in 1924, and your book is just one of many slated for publication. Suddenly your editor, Maxwell Perkins, gets sick and cannot write your flap copy. A junior editor, say, a gin-swilling Yale dropout who got his job through nepotism, is eager to do it; he just needs a day or two to read the manuscript. Clearly, you say no thanks, I'll do it myself.

Remember: no one knows this book like you do. (A good reason to have a few simpatico readers for input.)

How can your flap copy make this book alluring? Address the Big Questions. Whose story is it? Well, the title is the *Great Gatsby,* so there's no question of who is the central focus (though in this case the focus is not the narrator). What's at stake? Life and death, as it turns out, though you would not want to say that, and telegraph the end of the book. How you distill your story into flap copy will depend on what you want to emphasize:

> SCENE: You can start with an evocative *scene* suggesting the ambience, era, milieu, or major characters:
> Jazz, gin, and gorgeous strangers filled the night at Gatsby's mansion that summer Nick Carraway rented a cottage nearby.
> THEMATIC: You can start with a *thematic* statement:
> A story of love and loss, of corruption, and a grand though spurious dream. (Use your thematic statement either at the beginning or the end.)
> QUOTE: You can start with a *quote* expressive of the major characters and/or major thematic:
> "Her voice is full of money." Or, perhaps, "They were careless people." Or perhaps:
> "'You can't repeat the past.' I said.
> 'Can't repeat the past?' he cried incredulously. 'Why of course you can!'"

Your flap copy should have pith, info, and drama. The diction of your flap copy should echo the style of the story: Is yours a tender family memoir full of sweet tea and Shoo Fly Pie? Is it a bleak tale of deprivation seasoned with humor? Is it elegiac, or wistful, or jaunty? Is your story energetic, irreverent, a la Huck Finn's opening line, "You don't know about me, without you have read a book by the name of *The Adventures of Tom Sawyer*"?

Here is Sarah Jane Perkins's short flap copy for her memoir of a

Depression-era Skagit River childhood, *Perkins Finest*. Notice that she uses a quote and a scene and the thematic, all woven together in casual diction that suits her story. Note too her repetition of the title. Note too that she doesn't tell the whole story, but only alludes at the end to the drama and the challenges the family faced.

"This here hotel, it'll make you rich, Mr. Perkins." That's what Mr. Watson told my father when Pa bought Watson's Landing on the Skagit River, bought it dirt cheap in 1930. When my family moved into the hotel, Ma took over in the kitchen, and the food was awful and never got better. However, Pa built himself a nice little still on an island downriver. Here, using the lowly potato, he made bootleg hooch, Perkins Finest, vile stuff, by any standard, but much in demand during Prohibition. Watson's Landing did not make us rich, but Perkins Finest, gave us the only prosperity my family would ever know. This memoir tells the story of a riverbank honky-tonk childhood, of a crippled father who never lost his spirit, of a mother who never lost her spite, of a flood that came to kill, and left us homeless on the shoals of necessity.

## The Query Letter

Basically, the query letter is a three-paragraph tap dance. In contrast to the agonies of writing flap copy/synopsis, the query letter is much simpler, though it still has challenges. After all, you want to sound respectful but not grave. You want to sound lively but not cute. Do not try for irony; if it flops, you're finished. Keep your sentences short and to the point. Write well, and be absolutely certain of your spelling, grammar, and punctuation. If your letter looks random and sloppy, why would your book be any different? The query letter does not have to be a work of art; it has to make the book and author sound interesting, and lead the reader to the flap copy that will instill in that person a compelling desire to read the book.

## PARAGRAPH #1: INVITATION AND INTRODUCTION

Dear xxxx

I was delighted to see on xxxx.com that you (or xxxxx Agency) are accepting new clients. [Or here: If you have met this individual at a conference, mention that. Mention here if they have been suggested to you by a colleague or mentor.] Judging from your profile, I believe my book TITLE will appeal to your [literary? commercial? adventurous? astute? kinky? unique, if all else fails] tastes. [Add here if they represent a title or an author you think comparable to your work, or someone you vastly admire.] TITLE [here ally your story to a particular genre or a particular tradition.] [Finish with]: TITLE is a story of xxx xxx xxx [Just a few words. Flap copy will follow.]

## PARAGRAPH #2: THE AUTHOR BIO

A *short* description of yourself, *especially as your bio may reflect on the book itself,* work, education, family background. If you have particular credentials pertinent to the book, list them swiftly. You're not going on a date; you want them to read your flap copy. Get there. Do not tell a lot about yourself. You can do that later if they're interested. If you have publishing credits, this is the place to put them.

## PARAGRAPH #3: UNDERSCORING AND TRANSITION

I think TITLE AGAIN work will suit your agency style, and that it will be a title you'll be proud to represent. A description of TITLE AGAIN is below (not in an attachment, but right there following your signature).

I will hope to hear from you soon. I thank you in advance for your time and attention.

Name

Email

Phone with time zone and a link to your website if you have one. If they are interested they will probably check out the website; so it too should offer your best face forward—no pictures of your college hijinks.

My suggestion is to send these out in batches of five. Keep careful records of who responds with what. Many will not respond at all. Get used to it. If you don't hear in two weeks, you're probably not going to hear at all. Have another batch ready to go. This process can take months.

## An Alternate Possibility

Speaking of an author for whom time was of the essence, Peggy Kalpakian Johnson finished writing *Centennial Memoir* when she was ninety-seven years old. She had fulfilled her ambition to write a tribute to her immigrant parents, so she did not need to find an agent and a publisher in order to reap the satisfactions of her work. She did not want to deal with a lot of Internet obligations, or find book designers, or contract with proofers. She did not want the expense or the long timetable of a hybrid publisher. She never intended to sell the memoir in the bookstore or online. There is no e-book. It does not have an ISBN number. She wanted to have a book in hand, memory into memoir, and a party to celebrate.

We approached a local printing business, Threshold Documents, with whom we have dealt happily in the past, and moved ahead with Norman Green, the owner. We selected the photographs. We edited and proofed the text. Norm did the layout and formatting, including the many photographs, some of them difficult by virtue of age and in need of special treatment to show up on the page. Peggy chose the cover photo. Norm chose the typeface and designed the cover. We ordered two hundred copies. He had the books bound and delivered. He gave us a hundred bookmarks adorned with the cover photo. In short, we had the book printed rather than published.

On a July afternoon at a local Mediterranean deli and grocery store where the food is cooked on-site by two Lebanese sisters, we hosted an open house. Appetizers, wine, sunlight streaming through the windows, and Middle Eastern music wafting from unseen speakers.

My sister came up for the event, and she brought a little ceramic sign that said *Best Day Ever*. We put it on the table where Peggy signed copies of her book, and we sold *Centennial Memoir* for ten dollars a pop to a festive and admiring crowd. Indeed it was a Best Day Ever for my mom. We are all so proud of her, of her hard work, her dedication to this project and to the memory of her parents. I keep my signed copy of *Centennial Memoir* in a place of honor on the shelf with my own books.

# 13 | Truth

*O gentle Reader!* . . .
*What more I have to say is short,*
*And you must kindly take it:*
*It is no tale; but, should you think,*
*Perhaps a tale you'll make it*
—William Wordsworth, "Simon Lee," 1798

R eaders and writers subscribe to the belief that the author of the
memoir will not (or ought not to) falsify events, people, or situations. But in the act of picking up the pen, wrangling narrative
form over the often recalcitrant past, the author will edit for effect.
The very act of writing alters presentation, beginning with the creation of the narrator. Novelists may choose to tell the story through a
third-person narrator who can float at a distance from the people and
events described (that's why they call it fiction), but on leaving the
shores of fiction, we sail off not into "truth" but into nonfiction. Nonfiction is not truth, and memoir is not history. Memoir need not aspire
to history, certainly not such history as is written by sage, scholarly,
academic arbiters. Memoir leans more toward "story." Even the most
decorous and white-gloved sort of memoir is noisy, even unruly in a
way that history disdains. Memoir embraces not just the way things
happened, but the story the narrator weaves around what is remembered, and what that story means to the author. These elements bear
on one another. At crucial points, they are connected, and certainly
they are related, but they are always not the same tale. Truth is relative
to the teller.

The past is recollected in fractured, prismatic ways, different aspects to the same experience. In acknowledging the prismatic past,
some writers call into question the very nature of what they remember.
In *Oleander, Jacaranda*, one of my favorite memoirs, British writer

Penelope Lively describes her often lonely childhood in wartime Egypt where the family lived an opulent, colonial life; her father was a British official at the Bank of Egypt, and her mother was a socialite. Penelope was seven when World War II broke out. In her memoir she places fragments that she remembers against the reading she has done since, historical accounts of the war in Egypt, trying to ascertain if what she remembers is, so to speak, true; that is, historically correct. The two don't always tally, but her presentation is a fascinating take on the nature of memory. Early on in *Educated*, Tara Westover questions the recollections she has set down. She solicited responses from some siblings, who responded with often conflicting memories, and she briefly includes their versions in her book. She does not hand-wring over these disparities, nor lawyerlike whittle them into some semblance of an agreed-upon truth; she lets them stand. In bringing them up at all, she signals to the reader that she knows hers is not the whole story, and certainly not the whole truth, which is to say, she testifies to her own fallibility. There's a touching modesty in this admission, but throughout, her narrative voice is assured rather than self-effacing.

Each writer views the past through their own prism, and that coloration reflects upon the page. Sometimes that prism can be an emotion such as regret. Sometimes it can be a need for personal clarity. Sometimes it can be to highlight a relationship or an achievement. Sometimes it can be to re-create the sunny hours. Sometimes it can be to right a wrong.

Truth belongs to the teller, and to write the truth can require courage, especially if your memoir chronicles a coming out, a speaking out, a breaking away. If your memoir gives voice to the long unspoken, you will need your courage. The less the story conforms to happily-ever-after, the more strength will be obliged of the author. The more searing the truth, the more bravery will be required. The more the truth hurts, the more reason the author may have to unburden herself of that pain. The writer whose truth is trauma will be beset with perils. Writing means reliving. To write at all means coming to some sort of confrontation with that past. In my years of teaching I have worked with writers whose memoirs have left me humbled by the suffering they endured. And yet my task was, indeed is, to help these writers better present even unthinkable events.

The mind cannot resurrect the sensation of physical pain; that is, you can remember you were once in pain, but you cannot actually revisit that pain. But psychic, emotional pain lives on, easily reawakened and often devastating all over again, no matter the years that separate the person from what happened. I once worked with a writer whose tale was so terrible, so complex that there seemed no good place, certainly no obvious place to begin. She wrote about her childhood and youth, culminating in a series of devastating events when she was seventeen after which she left home and moved to a distant city. In the years following she went on to marry, to raise a child, successfully stifling these traumas. In her forties an incident sent her flying back; PTSD thrust her deep into that hellish past and left her throttled to the core, as if she were seventeen and defenseless all over again. In helping her cope with that remembered trauma, a therapist recommended she write it as a memoir. That is how she came to me. Beginning work on her memoir was indeed an act of bravery, a victory over everything and everyone—living and dead—who would keep her silent.

One of the challenges for the writer of a trauma memoir is that even if the author was utterly flattened, knocked senseless, on all fours, the narrator cannot be. The narrator must describe her ordeal, to offer context and insight, even introspection, into the circumstances that permitted trauma, abuse, cruelty. Cami Ostman—an author, a writing coach, and a professional therapist—sometimes counsels writers to render that experience in the third person, in effect, to take a step back to get the experience on the page. Sometimes altering the verb tense from present tense to past also can help the writer who must revisit trauma.

Some writers change the names to be better able to put the past on the page. If changing the names makes it easier for you to write, then change the names. When the book is published, there's usually a disclaimer page stating that some names have been changed (as Dani Shapiro does in *Inheritance*). Shannon Hager in *Five Thousand Brothers-in-Law*, the story of her marriage to a prisoner in Angola Prison, Louisiana, identified people with nicknames: Big Kidd, Boss Man, Baby Daddy, Baby Mama, Grandbaby, Patty Cake, and Home Girl. Changing the names does not fundamentally change the experience that's rendered—that truth still belongs to the teller—but it allows the author to take a step back.

The swamp of childhood can itself veil trauma where the individual didn't even recognize senseless cruelty when it was perpetrated upon him because, well, that's the way the world is. Kids only apprehend, conceive of values as they are lived within the family, in the school, in the neighborhood. Moving away from all that, into adulthood—sometimes moving physically away from that place—affords perspective, recognition. Anne Moody's powerful classic, *Coming of Age in Mississippi*, chronicles the narrator's growing awareness of the heavy hand of bigotry and oppression all around her. As Anne comes into young womanhood, she fights racism and segregation, putting her family in peril. Her narrator is not saying, *Look at me, how brave I am!* Her narrator is pissed off. Remains pissed off. Her narrator takes abuse from her immediate family, as well as the white world and the hated status quo. The book, published in 1968, was a well-aimed blow at the status quo.

The memoir offers up private truths. Once those private truths move outside the writer's mind, outside the writer's hand, outside the writer's computer, they become, in effect, public truths—whether or not they are published truths. They are open to discussion, contention, dissension. Within families, sometimes a good deal of discussion, a lot of contention, and much dissension.

In writing *In Search of Pink Flamingos*, Susan Greisen, a retired nurse and the daughter of Nebraska farm folk, told the story of her two years in Liberia with the Peace Corps. But the larger, deeper story here was of a young woman torn between the need for parental approval and the need to find her own adventurous path. Her parents emphatically did not approve of that path, and they let it be known. Her father was particularly blistering. Though her memoir balanced her father's bitterness and bigotry with instances of his physical bravery, Greisen created a harsh picture of his beliefs, his values, his words and actions. When she finished writing the book she sent it to her brother; she wanted him to know what she had said about their father. The brother's ringing endorsement of her portrayal permitted her to move forward with publishing.

Not all writers have that empowering experience. Whether they publish their books or not, if the manuscript is given to others in the family, more often than not word comes back: "That isn't the way it happened!" Often family members will significantly differ, not perhaps about the events themselves, but about what they meant, and how they are portrayed. "You're way too hard on Mom. She wasn't like that!" came the cry to one writer who sent her work to her sisters. The writer, surprised by their vehement reactions, reminded them that she was the eldest child, and that made her experience, her relationship with their mother, different than theirs. She did not alter what she had written. Her truth belonged to herself.

Sometimes in seeking a way to portray a larger truth, the writer may endow an incident with significance or insight that was not perhaps present at the time, a truth created to serve the narrative rather than slavishly adhere to the experience lived. One of the most graceful examples of this technique is an incident in *Angela's Ashes* where young Frankie is hospitalized. Recovered enough to be ambulatory, late one night Frankie finds his way to the deserted second floor of the hospital, and there amid the dim light and the long rows of empty beds he encounters the green-lipped ghosts of the Irish who died during the mid-nineteenth century famine, those poor starving wretches who were reduced to eating grass. McCourt's narrator remains the same unblemished Innocent as ever, but in creating these ghosts, the author is able to convey to readers the complex, haunting elements of Ireland's past, a collective memory without which Ireland, and, by extension, McCourt's book, cannot be fully understood. In terms of the most basic sort of "truth" (i.e., did this really happen?), I suspect the boy Frankie probably did go to the second floor, but the *adult author Frank* drew the ghostly, indeed ghastly inferences from that silence. The adult author portrayed the truth implied by those empty rows of beds. In doing so he gave his personal memoir a historical dimension essential for the reader, especially any reader unacquainted with Ireland's past.

In *Many Hands Make Light Work*, Cheryl McCarthy's sunny memoir of growing up in a family of nine children in Ames, Iowa, the author focuses on those lively, crowded years in which all nine kids lived at home. Naturally, over time, one by one her siblings moved out and moved on, but to chronicle that process would have grown tedious and boring. In her wisely crafted final chapter, McCarthy portrays a certain Christmas and described the family's Christmas traditions, lavishing on them the general affection everywhere present in the book. Toward the end of that scene she endows her narrator with insight created from retrospective nostalgia. The author, clearly, is looking back, but her *narrator looks ahead*, imagines the years as they pass and how all this will change: the family will not always be together and these Christmases, indeed, these years are the more precious because they will slide into the past. It's a lovely, fitting closure to a fond memoir.

The memoir is not the courtroom and not the confessional, and in the memoir there is no whole truth and nothing but the truth, so help you, God, or otherwise. Indeed, each writer decides how to approach the truths they want to describe. This does not render their memoir false; it means editing for effect.

*The Heart to Artemis: A Writer's Memoir* by Bryher is a good example of the author's right to portray the truth with self-imposed caveats. Born Winifred Ellerman, Bryher (1894–1983) endowed herself with this arresting single name, taken from an island. The name Winifred is mentioned only once in *The Heart to Artemis*, and her last name, Ellerman, never. She had a much younger brother, and his name is never mentioned. We are told her parents were able to marry when she was fifteen. Why they had not married before that? She offers no explanation whatsoever. Bryher repeatedly describes her family's values as decidedly middle class, but in truth she was the daughter of one of the richest men in England, a fact never mentioned. She was active in the artistic ferment of the 1920s in Europe and America, and she moved for decades among an array of interesting friends who make lively appearances here. Her lovers do not. However, she is candid about her two marriages of convenience (though telling nothing of the divorces, and little of the actual relationships). The American poet H. D. (Hilda Doolittle, 1886–1961) appears in these pages, but not as the love of Bryher's life, which she assuredly was. Nowhere will you read anything of the depth and complexity of their relationship, its rifts and rocky moments. In short, the contents of the book live up to the subtitle, "A Writer's Memoir": a story of travels, alliances, adventures, and nonromantic passions. Though I left her book more curious about Bryher than when I began, as a reader I admired the author's insistence on choosing her truths.

In Henry Adams's classic tome, *The Education of Henry Adams*, the author (1838–1918) lavishes his often opaque prose over a swath of incidents and individuals from his earliest memories as the grandson of one president, John Quincy Adams, and the great-grandson of a Founding Father, John Adams. Perhaps two-thirds of the way through, the narrative halts in 1872 and picks up again in about 1900, offering no comment whatsoever on the thirty-year hiatus. In 1872 Adams married Marion (Clover) Hooper, and in 1885 Clover committed suicide. Adams left all that, and his life with Clover, out of his narrative. The latter part of *The Education of Henry Adams*, after about 1900, is a sort of collective memoir about a cadre of friends, accomplished men of Adams's generation who came of age during the Civil War.

The past is, of necessity, shared with those who lived through it alongside us. This can include, as does Henry Adams, a broad generational cohort. Among one's contemporaries, this cohort can be people for whom, even if they share nothing else, music, movies, television shows, major historical events will "ping" like a tuning fork. People who lived through certain catastrophic events will always remember where they were when, say, John F. Kennedy was shot, or 9/11, or, for some, when Kurt Cobain died. The past can be shared with a regional cohort, like Rick Bragg's Arkansas memoirs, or a neighborhood as in Sarah Broom's lively *The Yellow House*. Even in the most intimate family memoir, the past cannot be wholly staked out like a claim, deeded to one individual.

Thus, some of the events my mother, Peggy Kalpakian Johnson, describes in *Centennial Memoir* also appear in a long memoir essay that I wrote, "Declarations and Denials." Neither of us experienced my grandparents' life in Adana, Turkey, their brief sojourn in Syria, their moving to Constantinople. None of the still extant family lived any of that, but it still belongs to us by way of family stories that commingle over time, as well as my grandmother's "The Story of My Life" written when she was in her eighties, typed by my aunt, stapled and sent to each of us. Some of that family history is a past my mother lived but was too young to remember: her infancy in Constantinople, the voyage to America, then to Greece, then back to America, and the early years at 905 Harding Avenue (though she does remember a particular gala 1926 wedding reception for an uncle and his bride). I can access Peggy Johnson's childhood and youth in Depression-era Los Angeles through her memories, and now, fortunately, through her memoir. We—all of us—have narrative access to what we cannot remember. It seems to me that, in general, the span of people's lives is not set by the dates on tombstones. Rather, our lives stretch from the oldest person we remember to those perhaps as yet unborn who will remember us, any life we touch, however obliquely, in which we are memorable. The poet and novelist Thomas Hardy (1840–1928) often based his work on tales told to him when he was just a lad, stories from people who had lived through the Napoleonic Wars. In "One We Know," dedicated to his grandmother who lived from 1772 to 1857, the last stanza reads:

She seemed one left behind of a band gone distant
So far that no tongue could hail:
Past things retold were to her as things existent,
Things present but as a tale.

———

In writing a memoir we each bring to the past a different prism of purpose. That prismatic past belongs to the writer alone. The prismatic past has a lovely rainbow ring to it, but there's another aspect to finding the truth in memoir, one made experientially vivid for me amid the muck and chaos when our basement flooded in 2010. Not a poetic moment.

Years earlier, in 1987, my grandmother had died and my parents, both retired by now, sold their home and moved north to live near me and my sons. Suddenly, I inherited two generations' worth of stability and furniture. Fortunate timing, since after years of restless renting, I had just bought this big house. When my parents moved north they loaded all their family memorabilia—picture albums, artifacts, letters, diaries, documents—into cardboard boxes and all that went into my basement where, amid all the other sorts of stuff one finds in basements, it sat undisturbed until December 2010.

In December 2010, near-biblical rains assaulted us, day after day, and water so inundated the basement that the only drain backed up. My youngest son, Brendan, and two of his friends, Tyler and Sean, came to help me face the catastrophe. For days these young men waded fearlessly in, armed with shovels and hoes, their hands sheathed in thick rubber gloves. They had T-shirts and bandanas tied around their faces to block the mold and mildew smell. The muck was made worse because long before we lived here someone had laid old, thick rag rugs in the basement. These were now soaked and disgusting. But before the lads could even use the shovels and hoes on the rugs, we had to slosh through and decide what was to be done with all this family stuff, soggy box by soggy box. What was precious and what was mere debris had fallen equally victim to the watery inundation. I had to decide was to be thrust into garbage bags and hauled up the outside steps to the ever-mounting pile of crap. And what could be saved or salvaged, put in laundry baskets, and go up the inside stairs to the second floor.

While the lads did the hauling I picked through the family flotsam and jetsam of decades. Much that should have been saved could not be salvaged. Of what could be salvaged, what should be saved? Some choices were obvious—what was ruined beyond any hope clearly had to go. Some were judgment calls that had to be made on the spot. I was going through my family's communal past, some of which was surprisingly touching, some that was puzzling, some that was weird. I felt a terrible responsibility that could not be shirked or reassigned. No time to ponder what this or that might mean or suggest. No time to question. No time to poke about. This goes outside. This goes upstairs.

My mother might have been moved to save or salvage items that I tossed, but she could not be there. My dad was very much afflicted with dementia, and as his sole caretaker she could not leave him alone. When I told my mom some of what I threw out, she couldn't even remember packing it up twenty years before. But some of it she sighed over. She didn't criticize or ask me to fetch it out of the enormous pile of crap we had to pay to have hauled away. But she sighed. I felt bad.

If ever there were another metaphor for truth in memoir, that yucky, mucky disgusting flooded basement is every bit as apt as the lovely prism. There's the reaching into the sludge and the pulling up, the choosing and the discarding, that's part of writing a memoir. There's the surprise of coming on what you thought had been lost forever. There's the chagrin of coming upon what you wish had been lost forever. There's the surprise of coming on material you had no idea even existed. There's the standard you use to rescue or discard. It's not simply a standard of sentiment, or even a standard of what is actually true (because the actual truth is always plural). The writer reaches down into the past and paws about, searching for whatever might be useable, even if it's incomplete, what might be significant even if it's enigmatic, what might be important even if it's painful. Over that, the author imposes narrative voice and structure, and in doing so, holds it up to the light. That's where the prism comes in, and the light shines through and the truth shines out like a rainbow.

———

FINI

# Works Mentioned

*Adventures of Huckleberry Finn* by Mark Twain

*Alice's Adventures in Wonderland* by Lewis Carroll

*The Alice B. Toklas Cookbook* by Alice B. Toklas

*All God's Dangers: The Life of Nate Shaw*
    by Theodore Rosengarten, editor

*All Over But the Shoutin'* by Rick Bragg (and other memoirs)

*American Cookery* by Laura Kalpakian

*Angela's Ashes* by Frank McCourt (and other memoirs)

*Anne of Green Gables* by L. M. Montgomery

*As You Like It* by William Shakespeare

*Autobiography of W. E. B. Dubois* by W. E. B. Dubois

*Autobiography of Havelock Ellis* by Havelock Ellis

*Autobiography of Malcolm X* by Malcolm X (finished by Alex
    Haley)

*Autobiography of Benjamin Franklin* by Benjamin Franklin

*Bartleby* by Herman Melville

*Between Them* by Richard Ford (and other memoirs)

*Beyond Belief: The Secret Lives of Women in Extreme Religions*
    edited by Susan Tive and Cami Ostman

*Borrowed Time* by Paul Monette

*The Cab at the Door* by V. S. Pritchett (and other memoirs)

*Cannery Row* by John Steinbeck

"The Car" by Raymond Carver (poem)

*Caveat* by Laura Kalpakian

*Centennial Memoir: A Tribute to My Parents*
    by Peggy Kalpakian Johnson

*Children of Pride* edited by Robert Manson Myers

*Coming of Age in Mississippi* by Anne Moody

*The Correspondence of F. Scott Fitzgerald* edited
   by Matthew Bruccoli et al.
*David Copperfield* by Charles Dickens
*The Crack-Up* written by F. Scott Fitzgerald
   and edited by Edmund Wilson
*The Delinquent Virgin* by Laura Kalpakian (stories)
*Diaries of Virginia Woolf* by Virginia Woolf
*Diary of Anna Green Winslow: A Boston Schoolgirl of 1771*
   edited by Alice Morse Earle
*Dictionary of Slang and Unconventional Usage* by Eric Partridge
*Eat Pray Love* by Elizabeth Gilbert
*Educated* by Tara Westover
*A Farewell to Arms* by Ernest Hemingway
*Five Thousand Brothers-in-Law* by Shannon Hager
*The Force of Things* by Alexander Stille
*The Gang: Coleridge, the Hutchinsons and the Wordworths in 1802*
   by John Worthen
*The Go-Between* by L. P. Hartley
*The Godfather* by Mario Puzo
*Graced Land* by Laura Kalpakian
*The Grapes of Wrath* by John Steinbeck
*Great Expectations* by Charles Dickens
*The Great Gatsby* by F. Scott Fitzgerald
*The Great Pretenders* by Laura Kalpakian
*Harry Potter* books by J. K. Rowling
*The Heart of This Family* by Linda Morrow
*The Heart to Artemis* by Bryher
*H is for Hawk* by Helen McDonald
*A House on Stilts: Mothering in the Age of Opioid Addiction*
   by Paula Becker
*The Hundred Mile Walk: An Armenian Odyssey*
   by Dawn Anahid MacKeen
*I, Tina* by Tina Turner

*In Search of Pink Flamingos* by Susan Greisen
*Inheritance* by Dani Shapiro (and other memoirs)
*Just Kids* by Patti Smith (and other memoirs)
*Kitchen Confidential* by Anthony Bourdain
*Letters of Virginia Woolf* by Virginia Woolf
*The Liars' Club* by Mary Karr (and other memoirs)
*Many Hands Make Light Work: A Memoir* by Cheryl McCarthy
*Martha's Mandala* by Martha Oliver-Smith
*The Memoir Club* by Laura Kalpakian
*Memoirs of U S Grant* by Ulysses S. Grant
*Moll Flanders* by Daniel Defoe
*The Music Room* by Laura Kalpakian
*My Family and Other Animals* by Gerald Durrell
*Negroland* by Margo Jefferson
*Notes of a Native Son* by James Baldwin
*Oleander, Jacaranda* by Penelope Lively (and other memoirs)
"One We Know" by Thomas Hardy (poem)
"People's Parties" by Joni Mitchell (song)
*Remembrance of Things Past* by Marcel Proust
*A River Runs Through It* by Norman McLean
*Roxana The Fortunate Mistress* by Daniel Defoe
"Simon Lee" by William Wordsworth (poem)
*A Small Boy and Others* by Henry James
*Speak, Memory* by Vladimir Nabokov
*So Much Depends* edited by Jessica Stone (anthology)
"Star-Spangled Banner" by Francis Scott Key (song)
*Stuffed: Adventures of a Restaurant Family* by Patricia Volker
*Sweet Thursday* by John Steinbeck
*Swimming with Monks* by Malachi McCourt
*A Tale of Two Cities* by Charles Dickens
*Tender at the Bone* by Ruth Reichl
*Tender is the Night* by F. Scott Fitzgerald
*These Latter Days* by Laura Kalpakian

*Three Strange Angels* by Laura Kalpakian

*To Kill a Mockingbird* by Harper Lee

*Tom Sawyer* by Mark Twain

*Tortilla Flat* by John Steinbeck

*Twopence to Cross the Mersey* by Helen Forrester
    (and other memoirs)

*Up From Slavery* by Booker T. Washington

*Where the Wild Things Are* by Maurice Sendak

*Wild* by Cheryl Strayed

*The Woman Warrior* by Maxine Hong Kingston

*The Yellow House* by Sarah Broom

# Acknowledgments

A big round of gratitude to my writing students over the years. Thank you for trusting me and one another with your stories. I have learned so much from so many of you.

Thank you to the University of Washington for the opportunity to serve as Theodore Roethke Writer-in-Residence, and to the students in English 581, especially Judy Sobeloff, Martha Silano, Lang Cook, Richard Burns, Morgan Kellock, Laura Gamache, Alison McLean, Svenja Soldovieri, and Susie Freehafer.

Thank you to Andrea Sigler-Castro, Jane Hodges, Resa Moore, and Jayne Sprinkle, teaching assistants and dear friends. Thank you to Mary Alice Sanguinetti, Jamie Wilson, and Martha Oliver-Smith, who has been my writing amiga even before we were writers. Belated gratitude to Kit Ward who always wanted me to write a memoir, to Charlotte Bonica who opened her lovely home to that first independent memoir group, and to Aileen Boustedt. Gratitude to Seattle's reigning writing guru, Priscilla Long. Thank you to Muriel Dance and to Carol Nicolay for giving me the opportunity to teach these classes.

Muchos gracias to reading and writing amigos and amigas, Cami Ostman, Pam Helberg (both have been after me for years to write this book), Tele Aadsen, Andrea Gabriel, Janna Jacobson, Frances Howard-Snyder, Victoria Doerper, Connie Feutz, Jolene Hanson, Carol McMillan, Susan Chase-Foster, Jes Stone, Lisa Dailey, Joe Nolting, Linda Morrow, Roy Taylor, Nancy Taylor, Cheryl McCarthy, and Kate Miller. Thank you to that loose affiliation of lively compatriots, The Red Wheelbarrow Writers, who have created a supportive, sustaining writers' alliance.

Ongoing gratitude to my wonderfully supportive family: my mother, Peggy Kalpakian Johnson; my sister, Helen Johnson; my sons, Bear and Brendan McCreary; and to Raya Yarbrough.

Thanks to Elise McHugh and the staff of the University of New Mexico Press for bringing this book into being.

Ongoing gratitude to my literary agents, Pamela Malpas and Juliet Burton, for believing in my work.

Much applause to Andrea Gabriel of Creekside Collaborative for creating and maintaining my website, laurakalpakian.com. Readers can find here additional resources for *Memory into Memoir* including the reading list from English 581 and reviews of many of the books in "Works Mentioned," and the first three chapters of Peggy Johnson's *Centennial Memoir*.

My own book of memoirs, *The Unruly Past: Memoirs* has been published by Paint Creek Press. Paint Creek has also re-issued several of my earlier works, including *These Latter Days* and *The Memoir Club*, from which Sarah Jane Perkins's excerpts have been taken. These are available as trade paperbacks or ebooks through the Paint Creek website or your independent bookstore, or wherever you buy books.